D1516378

A MIRROR FOR
ANGLO-SAXONS

A MIRROR FOR ANGLO-SAXONS

A Discovery of America,
A Rediscovery of England

by

MARTIN GREEN

Harper & Brothers, Publishers
New York

Grateful acknowledgment is made to Mr. Robert Graves for
permission to reprint "Superman on the Riviera" from *Food
for Centaurs,* published by Doubleday & Co., Inc. Copyright ©
1959 by Robert Graves.

The lines quoted on pages 18 to 22 are from *Manners for Mil-
lions* by Sophie C. Hadida. Copyright © 1932, 1950, 1956 by
Sophie C. Hadida. Reprinted by permission of Doubleday &
Company, Inc.

Parts of this book first appeared in *Harper's Magazine, Kenyon
Review, Partisan Review* and *Quixote.*

Library of Congress catalog card number: 60-10405

To My Mother and Father

CONTENTS

A MIRROR FOR
ANGLO-SAXONS

When I got a job for the first time, in 1951, when I was twenty-three, it was as an assistant in a French school. Thanks to a series of scholarships and two years of military service, this was my first autonomous act—the first time I had earned my living, the first time I had chosen my place in the world. And its main attraction was that it was abroad. My friends thought they understood this wanderlust; they approved it. One naturally wanted a certain cosmopolitanism; Britain was where to live, but to remain civilized, one must draw periodically on Continental sources of life; France, Paris— night-long, eager conversations in boulevard cafés—Paris was where civilization began, where people knew how to live. One wanted, they knew, while one was still young, a certain amount of adventure and experience of a civilized kind—the kind useful to a civilized man. My friends were only surprised that it should be I rather than they who so actively sought adventure. But the centrifugal impulse doesn't have to be strong to take effect when the centripetal impulse is weak. I was the one for whom England was exerting least holding power. And that, though my friends would have been shocked to hear it, was the crucial factor in my great decision.

At the time, of course, I did not say this to myself. It was a secret from me as much as from them. I did not know what

"England" was—this book is the record of my finding out. At the time my dim, depressed restiveness could only be explained as something wrong with me. It could only too easily be explained that way, of course; there are always cousins and neighbors ready with that kind of explanation.

And I was only too conscious of not fitting in with what, at the time, I could only describe as life, or, at narrowest, society. I would not have believed that any concept so abstract and limited as "England" could be affecting me in such intimate and general feelings; feelings about what a friend expected from you when he recounted his love affairs, about your sherry-party posture and voice production, the carrying of an umbrella, and the wearing of a silk muffler tucked inside your shirt collar. Much less, of course, did I realize how responsible England was for my nonfeelings. And yet how could I feel any enthusiasm for becoming, say, a teacher, when no one had ever taught me, or anyone else I knew of, anything that really deeply mattered? I had seen a lot of good teaching at my school, and some real education, but it had all been in this one direction, of "England," of making one "English," and that could have no exciting and liberating effect for me, since it was just "England" I wanted, unconsciously, to be freed from. I mean that the ultimate educational effect of this good teaching had been to make the students one or other variety of that Englishman I myself didn't much enjoy being. So I had no enthusiasm for that; I had small enthusiasm for any career.

So I went to France, to the Collège Moderne et Technique in Fourmies, a quiet little town in the Département du Nord. Of course, I didn't find what my friends had promised. There were a couple of bright young teachers there, unhappily exiled from Paris, and I read a good deal of current French literature; I think I found the France I had come for—I certainly didn't "find" Fourmies—but it seemed no better a place to live in than England. Quite dull, decent people speculated quite dryly on what would replace the present national constitution or the present map of Europe; when the franc's exchange value fluctuated, my fellow teachers, with unemotional unself-conscious despair, predicted the total collapse of the currency and the government; there was a massive split, right through the very dining rooms and bedrooms of the town, between the Catholic Church and all its social organs, on the one side, and the Communist mayor and municipality on the other; one group of families was divided against another in a vendetta deriving from some alleged betrayal in the Resistance movement under the Occupation. And this crisis-filled atmosphere, to my sense, overstimulated and undernourished every ordinary domestic affection and relationship. It gave an El Greco distortion to every sensitive mind, while the life of the intellectuals seemed to me, after England, appallingly adrift and self-limited, a party of paddle boats bobbing about in mid-Atlantic. (In this French sense, I suppose, England has no intellectuals to compare; but we have something else; we have a tradition—though it is obscured for the moment—of integrating the most powerful intellectual faculties into an all-round, responsible human personality.) French intellectual life had for me the character of a continued holiday from bourgeois domesticities and duties; and the moral rigors of men like Sartre and Gide seemed like private gymnastics, whereby they worked up an exhaustion so they could sleep at night. I did not linger long over, I had scarcely even come for, those quiet old fishing hotels where the art of living (gentle, sensual, somewhat roguish) is so juicily practiced; or that earthy gaiety and amoral passion of Provence, where Nature apparently performs her own leukotomies. I was looking for somewhere with lots of closet space; where I could install all the old scruples and inhibitions I'd had since a child; I wouldn't feel the same without them.

3

So at the end of the year I was ready to leave France, but reluctant to go back to England; I decided to try America. It was more or less in these terms, this tone, that I put it to myself; a tone as of a man juggling three enormous black-painted, gas-filled, rubber dumbbells, loudly inscribed "Lead." For, let me repeat, the real damage England had done me was to diminish, nearly to repeal, that law of gravity which alone makes a moral life feasible. Self-commitment, to this or that, was too easy for me. France or America, capitalism or socialism, the intellectual life or the commercial, both alternatives in each case seemed quite possible and attractive. England had explained the different forms of life to me very clearly, but in a way that emptied them of color, weight, magnetism. They were all good in their way; all accidental products of social and historical forces; I could not help remembering that they might so easily have been different. These huge bulks of moral and material fact were light and maneuverable to my touch; I had comically little feeling of their reputed weight and mass; everything would change places without much effort. I could go to America or not; it didn't matter. I could cross the Atlantic Ocean, to another continent, another culture, leave behind everything I had known. Or not. It wasn't a big decision for me.

I got a job at the University of Michigan as a Teaching Fellow for a year. Halfway through, for a variety of reasons, I decided to stay another year, and by the end of that I was working for a Ph.D., and stayed a third. What I thought, or rather, at the time, felt, about America, will come out later in the book, particularly in the first, second, and fourth essays. I found myself in a nation where everyone expected things to get better; expected to be richer in ten years' time than they were at present, individually and collectively; and the riches were not merely material. Of course, intelligent people did not believe in progress, in any simple sense; but they hoped—that was the differ-

4

ence. And they believed, too, not in progress or any other idea, but in what they might become, individually and collectively, and with an intensity that made the air quite different in Ann Arbor from what it had been in Fourmies or Cambridge. I found myself feeling that what they believed in, as well as their state of belief, was genuinely exciting; and I sensed how satisfying it must be to have to choose between their alternatives, which were immovably solid and looming and irregular. Every aspect of life took on, gradually, the savor and luster and odor, the fine grainy roundness or knottedness which I at last realized it should have had always, had had for the heroes of the novels I had read.

It didn't occur to me, then, however, to settle down in America. These were my friends' alternatives and my friends' beliefs, though they made me see what such things were. I was excited and satisfied for them; for myself I had to find other alternatives and beliefs, British ones. A man can never belong to another place as intimately and radically as to the society in which he spent his first fifteen years. Tell me you like my wife in a British accent and I'll be ten times more excited, grateful, resentful, or suspicious than if you sang it beneath my midnight window in American. One can never replace that connection with another one as good; a man whose work lies with ideas and feelings, much less. The best thing about America, for me, was that it sent me back to England. I was very reluctant to leave my job and my friends in Ann Arbor, and the very palpable total ambiance, America, but I was also sure, in an undemonstrable, unrationalizable way, that I wanted to go home. I was pulled both ways, and how pleased I was with that. This was a human predicament, not the nightmarish lunar freedom I had had before. Everything had mass and solidity. I had to calculate my lifting powers, and give up one ambition to realize another.

Naturally I was very excited about this, in a pretty confused

5

way. But I couldn't get anyone to listen when I tried to talk about this discovery, this resurrection, this Lazarus-returned feeling. They all interrupted in their different ways, even those who only smoked and smiled, to reinterpret my paradoxical complexities into the broad general truths they could see written all over me. My French and British friends both had been very understanding, from the beginning, in 1952, replying to my first enthusiastic letters. They could perfectly sympathize with the aesthete's relish for vulgarity, the intellectual's curious sense of release in a society where no one had ever thought of thinking. They only reproached me for the obstinacy with which I refused to recognize that America is in the long run equally impossible, because it is already decadent as well as immature —"the only country to pass from unripeness to rottenness without an intervening stage." It is the West *that is in decline. My American friends, on the other hand, were so impressed with the complexity of their own complex fate that they felt an Englishman's complaints were rather out of place. (I'd like to say here, and I hope what follows supports this, that though it is a complex fate to be an American, it's much more so nowadays to be an Englishman or Frenchman; to be a Turk or a Portuguese, at the level of intelligence and sensibility we are assuming, is just about impossible. Comparatively, Americans have a simple fate.) They could only conclude I was dazzled, as a child of the lower classes, by my first glimpse of a truly democratic society.*

I hope this book will bear me out that what I discovered was really and truly not any new version of those old chestnuts. I was, and am, sure that what I had found in America, and what I, therefore, for the first time, discovered the lack of in Britain, is what made all the difference between that dull, dim, echoing, frightening weightlessness and the sense of eagerness and effort and choice and achievement. It is a matter of the dominant

6

images round which the cultural life of each country is organ-
ized. But I had not worked this out for myself then, in 1955,
and I was quite unable to convey to my friends the fragmentary
insights out of which I later built my discovery.

It was not, of course, my inability even to communicate with
other people conversationally on the subject that led me to
write about it, though that did continually rereveal, reillumin-
ate its urgency for me. I was not even sure what the subject was,
then. You'll see that in this first piece, which I wrote in the
garden at home in the summer of 1955, in the month or two
I was there, my conscious mind had no clear grasp of what was
agitating it. All it wanted to do was to offer some sprightly re-
marks on the two countries. It even wanted to be balanced and
dispassionate about them both, though I think it's clear enough
that there is a tendency in the piece, and what that tendency is.
I have rewritten this considerably, especially replacing the last
section about America with something a little less trite, but
I've tried to remain true to both the form and the inspiration
of the original piece.

HOME THOUGHTS FROM
ABROAD AND VICE VERSA

I

All England has an unfortunate air of being preserved—a mild green gherkin in cloudy spirits—but the Cunard ships beat everything that way. They are, as it were, the miniature, memento, cracker-trophy version, with a pretty little gherkin just perceptibly bobbing in the bottle. The *Ivernia* was a new ship, on its maiden voyage, but already old-fashioned, old-maidish, and quite consciously so. It might have been built to recapture the spirit of the past—perhaps the lower-middle-class twenties or—since it is after all true to the present too, the present England *being* essentially old-fashioned—it might have been reconstructed to the specifications of future archaeologists to stand in a museum room of the fifties.

The decorations have a sprightly modernity about them, rather gallant—"if that's what the young people want," as it were. Having achieved some effect with stripes on projecting parts of the wall they fill in the panels with crosses, and the ceiling, sometimes, with plaster garlands. The effect is indescribably fussy and cottagey.

The amusements are would-be rakish, rather than would-be modern. There is gambling morning, noon, and night; Tote in

8

the morning, Bingo in the afternoon, and Bingo in the evening. Shilling flung recklessly after shilling, to the purser's racy humor. Mr. Heinz's number, fifty-seven, five seven; Betty Grable's number, double one, the legs. Betty Grable, in 1955, the era of Marilyn Monroe! You'd almost think, wouldn't you, that there was a ten-year cultural time lag between the two countries? In a sense there is, but it's not that the films or the stars' publicity reaches England any later or in less quantity. It's that we can't respond to them, in this confidently public way, while they are fully contemporary and real. They are too vulgar, too alien, until time has diminished and tamed them a bit. Marilyn Monroe will be funny in another ten years. What a mummified, ritualistic sense of humor. Of course, there must always be limits and conventions, but these are too rigid, too unnatural; humor and propriety should define themselves like a tide mark on sand, with a shifting, recurrent, irregular line. Not a stone wall. And the purser, a quick-stepping, square-shouldered thirty-year-old, with sharp, neat, yellow hair, smart in every sense, what is he thinking and feeling, day after day, voyage after voyage? His private sense of humor, if he is at all in touch with people his own age, must be so different. But, being British, he has to pretend to live half in the past. An American purser also no doubt leads an unreal life, seen always in a pseudo-romantic light, but at least his pseudo romance is in a contemporary mode. At least he can see his life, dramatized in the movies, looking really glamorous.

Then when the Get-Together Dance begins we play Musical Chairs, with the men's knees for chairs. Shrieks go up when the idea is announced, people are literally holding their sides before the dance is over, and one overhears—in the cool of reflection the next day—"Well, I never heard of *that* before." They feel really giggly and blushy about it. Of course, the people on this trip were predominantly middle-aged or oldish (English people almost entirely, though some had lived quite a few years in Canada) and everyone's idea of sexual humor seems to go haywire as he grows older. But Musical Chairs, surely, belongs to the past for everyone, nowadays. It is not a contemporary, not a fully real thing. And all the possible variations, it seems to me, one has heard of, or could hear of without emotion. These people had been through marriage, and childbirth, the whole sexual cycle. Standing at the railing, overhearing, one felt something heave and swell and tug at its moorings inside one.

Anyway, to counterbalance this rakishness, there is food for the heart. Afternoon tea music, in the Amber Lounge, played by the Ivernia Sextet. "Because," "Always," "Tipperary," the sextet from *Floradora*, "My Old Dutch," and so on. A pretty little woman in a blue hat, smiling consciously, alone, fifty, her handbag in her lap and her too veined hand clutching a lace handkerchief on the chair arm, swinging her foot dutifully, but clumsily; out of time to the music. And across the room, writing letters, two exchange schoolteachers, in their twenties, going home after a year in Canada, identical sporty kerchiefs over their hair. They look and talk quite a bit like American college girls, from an Eastern college. But one suddenly catching a bit of a tune, her chin went up, her eyes to the side, she nudged the other; they were suddenly English, London-secretaryish; and the effect was to diminish them, to relegate them to a subordinate role.

On Sunday comes food for the soul, when the captain holds a religious service; the good old hymns, with the good old tunes, and memories, memories, memories. The Communion Service was attended by eight, all first-class passengers and unmistakably County; those round gray felt hats and round honest pink faces, listening to the Authorized Version, the Oxford accent, and the ecclesiastical cadence. The British captain and the British clergyman are both figures we have to refer back to a pre-1914 original to understand and respond to. There have been no glamorous versions since.

The whole trip was acutely disturbing. A band of dead souls chugging cheerfully and efficiently straight across the Atlantic.

Unluridly dead, in the English manner, just inoffensively un-
alive.

Life, nowadays, has an exclusively American accent.

II

On the other hand, one would hate to be an American. For
one thing, they are the most pharisaical nation in the world. Both
their present high prosperity and their original Land-of-Liberty
gesture force them into a moral stance which they all, in varying
degree, know is absurd. The gap between what they think they
are and what they really are is more cruelly ludicrous than the
equivalent in other countries. Partly because the audience, for
instance the foreign visitor, is more keyed up and ready to
laugh, but mostly because the actors are. There is more belief
in the air in America. Everyone inevitably jumps higher because of it, and falls harder.

To take one simple example, consider the split between the
two ideas of America, the division which runs down the middle
of the minds of all students in the Mid West, at least.

The first America is the land of the free and the home of the
brave, where men stride recklessly out into the unknown, carve
their own futures, make and enforce their own laws; men of
strength not grace, power not culture; Whitman, Mark Twain,
the frontiersman, the pioneer, the immigrant. In the Mid West
and West the young man, in his blue jeans and crew cut, can
still feel that he represents something simpler, bigger, better,
than his European equivalent. He is still in a special sense the
heir of honesty, adventure, self-assertion without privilege or
protection.

The other America believes that man's chief end is to glorify
society, to adapt himself to the world as he finds it, to achieve
security and solidarity. The aim of life is the happiness one
achieves psychologically by setting oneself a goal—any goal—
and achieving it, and sociologically by receiving the approba-
tion of the majority. In practical terms, this is the same kind of
happiness. Nor is this just a subterranean motion of prudence

and self-protection; it is an explicit policy, propagated by the educational system of the country, plus ten thousand columnists and commentators in newspapers, magazines, radio, TV, the movies, all the way up to Dr. Norman Vincent Peale. Only have faith and all shall be well; but not faith in anything; just sheer faith, the sheer affirmative exertion of the will, closing the eyes and crisping the muscles.

These two nations have much in common. Both are averse to metaphysics, to aesthetics, to any tragic view of history. Both exalt the will over the intelligence—all things not quantified and factual are equally unknowable, so that all intellectual argument (about literature or religion, say) is either polite conversation or indecent personal propaganda. So much is true of the whole class, except for the very superior student, but this unity only sets the stage for quite savage internal conflicts which each becomes aware of when he reads, for instance, *Death of a Salesman*. Willy's quandary is his own. Should he follow his brother Ben, and be lawless, self-dependent, a builder, or his wife Linda, and be well liked, limited to his social function, a salesman? These are the two Americas in Willy's mind, each seeming right, but incompatible together. Again, most students will confess, if pressed, that the colonists of 1776, if we look at their problems practically, as if they were ours today, were wrong to rebel. They were full of unadjusted idealism. And yet they know the colonists were right. They believe that too, very sincerely, if they can come at the problem from a historical and patriotic and theoretical point of view. As for Emerson and Thoreau, it is difficult to get most students nowadays to believe that these textbook heroes said what they did or meant what they said, so preposterous does it seem to them. And yet, find the right line, the right passage for them, and their faces will flush, they will be really stirred by that same idealism.

This is only one example of the involuntary American hypocrisy which appears whenever they talk about nature, or art, or politics, or the class system, or Europe; a hypocrisy which is much more rank and glaring than anything you find in Europe.

Culture is difficult to define, but it must have something to do with those habits of mind which control the quality of our thinking and feeling; the habit of laughing at certain things, taking some solemnly, others sentimentally, and the syndromes of those habits that are encouraged in a particular time and place; the ideal forms of love and laughter and energy which are held up for our admiration and to which we try to assimilate ourselves.

And when we use the word as a positive value, when we say someone lacks culture, we must mean, unless we're content to be snobs, that these habits in them are bad. They find funny, perhaps, people they too simply don't understand and are afraid of; they take solemnly things they don't, fairly palpably, believe in; they aim at a manner inappropriate to the facts of their situation.

Now most Englishmen, when driven to it—and we are all driven to it nowadays by the world situation—will admit they feel superior to Americans because Americans lack culture. What they are thinking of (when they don't mean Hawaiian shirts and gum and "Hey Bud") is that a typical good British film is, say, *Hamlet* or *Henry V,* while a typical good American film would be *On the Waterfront* or *From Here to Eternity.* A typical good British actor is Sir John Gielgud, a typical good American actor is Marlon Brando. What they don't realize is that from a cultural, as distinguished from an aesthetic, point of view, the British entries have practically nothing to offer. The syndrome of qualities Gielgud embodies and glorifies, through most of his parts—let's call it gentlemanliness—though charming, is hardly exciting; we've seen it all before, and arranged and labeled and priced the same way; we feel we've scarcely seen anything else. As for Shakespeare, his cultural values have got transmuted, by the process of time, into material for the textual annotators and the Elizabethan-world-picture writers. The forms of love and laughter he presents are no longer recognizable in the world around us. All that is left of his original meanings are the purely aesthetic ones. "Shakespeare as a cultural value" means only that it is a good *habit* to read great works, because, quite apart from what you realize you are getting out of them, it gives a kind of patina to your personality. Whereas in *On the Waterfront* we got an exact, explanatory rendering of a specifically contemporary reality (tones of voice, gesture, clothes, as well as buildings, movement, lighting) and the evolution of a moral and aesthetic order out of this chaos of unnamed detail. If Gielgud's Cassius was better than Brando's Antony in the film *Julius Caesar,* still Brando was far better there, in alien territory, than Gielgud would be in, say, *On the Waterfront.* Both are brilliant actors, but while the Englishman's talent works within relatively isolated conventions, social and aesthetic, the American is helping us to see, to hear, to respond to, the people in the street and in other streets we don't go down; to see them, also, with admiration and sympathy; to respond to them simply, unself-consciously, forgetting our differences. Nothing could be more acutely and valuably cultural.

Or let us take literature. In *The Catcher in the Rye* again you have a brilliant rendering of an idiom and a world both totally new and unevaluated, and so presented that a hundred new values come to life in the mind of the reader, new perspectives and perceptions sharpen themselves in every sentence. You learn to recognize the words and phrases and rhythms (to take only verbal behavior) that betray the differing failures of feeling in the prep school girl, the cab driver, the schoolteacher, the intellectual, etc; you recognize the *living* language when it comes in them, the words and phrases which, in that time and place, express unforced, unself-conscious understanding and sympathy; you recognize all the glory of a really creative idiom in the principal character's adolescent slang. What is there in England to compare with that? Perhaps we can take *The Portrait of the Artist as a Young Dog* as a fair example, and what the comparison immediately brings out is Dylan Thomas's renunciation of all the ordinary forms of responsibility in favor of the aesthetic; he condones, if he is conscious of it, the moral irresponsibility of the central character, and he feels, in his rendering of other persons and things, no fidelity to any general truth in them, beyond a minimal recognizability. From a cultural point of view, therefore, he has only occasional flashes of insight to offer, disjointed and at low pressure. Different as they are, Gielgud and Thomas bear the same testimony to the arts in England; that they have retreated from cultural responsibility.

It seems, then, that we have been confusing the cultural with the aesthetic. Or you could say that we have been confusing the imagination with the fancy. If a work of imagination must have moral size and energy and wholeness, and the fancy is an affair of wit, elegance, fantasy, then obviously it is in the latter that England can think herself superior. We have Alec Guinness and *Kind Hearts and Coronets;* we have *Orlando* and *Cold Comfort Farm.* This is what we have been meaning by culture. I think America could offer some competition there, and claim superiority in things like musical comedy, but that quarrel is not urgent. What is urgent is to recognize that works like *On the Waterfront* and *The Catcher in the Rye* represent their own kind of cultural triumph, unless we abandon culture to Angela Thirkell and Edith Sitwell. Is that perhaps what we have done?

IV

It does seem to me as if affairs in England have taken a definite turn toward the feminine during the years I have been away. The thing that strikes me most is the immense increase in gossip and snobbery in the newspapers. I grew up during the war, of course, and even up to 1951 it seems as if both the shortage of newsprint and the urgency of the national situation kept the proportion of fashion show, garden party, hunt ball, divorce talk down to a decent minimum in the papers. Nowadays the *Daily Express* is a good third made up of regular columns dealing with the social doings of the royal family, the peerage, fashion models, actors, jockeys, debutantes. (This same new interest in gossip, at a higher intellectual level, is presumably also to be seen in the postwar novels of Anthony Powell, Nancy Mitford, Evelyn Waugh, and the recent boom in Proust.) William Hickey's column in the *Daily Express,* for instance, which I remember as a series of fairly lightweight but conceivably masculine opinions, is now entirely in a feminine mode—now seems to be written by a woman. Half the news stories, presented in prim, tea-table manner, with pleasant photographs, deal with ex-colonial governor sexagenarian baronets caught sunbathing in the nude with the manageress of the local dress shop, or a rabbit-toothed vicar snapped through the window of the Dartmoor cottage where he is living in obstinate sin with a sixteen-year-old bespectacled choirgirl. " 'I Will Never Leave Harold,' says Anne." Matter and manner both are redolent of tea-party scandalmongering.

The BBC, of course, never sinks that low in matter, but its manner of avoiding vulgarity is equally feminine on a higher social level. Genteel, respectable, and responsible, it is always trying to raise our tone. Take for instance "Round Britain Quiz," a weekly competition between local teams in pretty much the same kind and degree of erudition as "64,000 Dollar Question" and the more intellectual American quiz shows. The British show offers no prizes, works up no artificial tension; it is on the radio, so there are no booths, no close-ups, no personal histories, the competitors merely say "Hello" or "I'm so and so" when they are introduced. Though each is something of a specialist, primarily they are all educated men, all equals, and they rally each other and the question master throughout the program in the spirit of scholarly equality; they are, as it were, overheard by the audience instead of quiz-master and audience together making the competitors jump through hoops to numbers, as in the American show. "Round Britain Quiz" is, I suppose, more one's own kind of entertainment, but "64,000 Dollar Question" is much *better* entertainment. The crudity, the cruelty, the vulgarity, do after all add up to excitement; and

16

to relaxation; you cannot *relax* with "Round Britain Quiz" because every one is behaving so beautifully. As a matter of fact, you cannot enjoy "Round Britain Quiz" even for the tepid, too-well-bred thing it is, because of its offensive confidence that the whimsey-laced learning it parades is wisdom, is culture, is education. Those port-wine voices, shrill or gruff, soaked in a sweet, rich arrogance of caste, identifying lines from *Alice in Wonderland*—this in England is deeply offensive and mischievous. One feels the need to protest, to dissociate oneself. It is brother or sister to the Sherlock Holmes game and the whole detective-story-reading line of clergymen and dons.

My point is that this governessy refinement and upliftingness characterize the BBC, which is both the most powerful of British cultural institutions, and the most representative of the others. It controls very much, for instance, the kind and quantity of feeling we have about the national sports, by the fact that most people's experience of football or cricket is that mediated through the well-bred tones of a BBC commentator. As for its representativeness, consider the royal family's public role, and you will see with what governessy refinement that works to satisfy, or pacify, appetites the Establishment does not really approve of. I mean that Princess Margaret and Prince Philip are offered to the public as glamorous idols (with a degree of prepared publicity that can be compared to nothing in America but that given to film stars, say, to Grace Kelly and Cary Grant), but that the glamour remains essentially well bred and, as it were, unconscious of the public, so that the latter gets a rather snubby lesson in good behavior as well as the thrill it came for. British cultural institutions, that is, try to give the public what it wants, monarchy, vaudeville, sports, scandal, strip-tease, but at the same time to smear a little uplifting powder into the jam. The daily news is read to the nation in a voice that is not more correct but more genteel than that used by 99 per cent of the listeners on their best behavior. And when what the public wants is something earthy, there's likely to be no jam at all; all through my adolescence one of the big Saturday night programs was "BBC Music Hall," where one of the biggest turns was that Rabelaisian figure, Joyce Grenfell.

It is a natural consequence, I'd suggest, of this feminization, that so many personalities in the public eye affect eccentricities —Peter Ustinov, Robert Morley, Gilbert Harding. They are driven to affectation because there is not enough room for self-assertion in the masculine role as socially defined. To be merely a man is too nearly to limit yourself to the scope of Sir Anthony Eden or Lord Attlee. Young men do not know how to become individual without becoming eccentric, in a feminine society.

V

However, in this matter too America has no advantage over us.

One of the big American myths it took me longest to understand from the inside was the polar opposition between America and Europe in which the former stood for Refinement and the later for Culture (and Sophistication). We meet this in Henry James's novels, of course, but I was never able to objectify it and feel it for myself until I came across *Manners for Millions*. This "Complete Guide to Courteous Behavior," issued by Barnes and Noble, as Number 233 in their Everyday Handbook Series, should be made available at reduced prices to all immigrants. For though it is much more alien and embarrassing to most Americans than to a European, it is so because they recognize in it a ghost they half-believed in, were half-aware of, in their childhood. I sense this book as a raven on the shoulders of the grade school teachers, counselors, dancing and deportment instructors, and bossy aunts of my students and my friends here. It is a part of the American heritage; the woman-oppressed part.

The chapter entitled "Odors," for instance, begins: "Do you smell sweet? Not with perfumes, powders, bath salts, pomades —oh no! Sweet with a clean odor that advertises your habit of the daily bath. EVERY DAY! EVERY DAY! EVERY DAY!" Those capitals and exclamation marks, that repetition, echo faintly in every American mind. Adolescents, and adolescent

18

boys above all, are to be especially careful about odors. Their glands are extra-active; they seldom realize how objectionable they are. The chapter covers several kinds of odor, some one hadn't thought of before, and by the time he has finished reading no one is sure how objectionable he is being. It breathes an unchallengeable confidence in the importance of its message, and extends that importance, with no sense of paradox, to touch most of life. "B.O. has been the cause of rupture of friendships, of the breaking of engagements, of exclusion from definite social groups, of disgusted expressions of the face, of quarrels between husbands and wives, friends, brothers and sisters— and how unnecessary—when for ten cents the difficulty can be removed." The marks that anxiety and that discipline leave on the face are part of the American expression.

There are several other chapters of that kind—Chapter 11, "Expectorating (Spitting)"; Chapter 12, "Picking"; Chapter 13, "Belching"; 14, "The Sniffler and the Snorter"; 15, "The Moistened Finger"; 16, "Hands Off!"; and of course "The Bathroom" and "The Handkerchief." Both the most ceremonious "daintiness" and the most circuitous avoidance of germs are prescribed, though it is perceptibly the former which is the more important. "The Birthday Cake" begins: "Now it's time to eat the birthday cake. Let's all blow out the candles. Blow! Blow! Blow! They're all out, and so are the germs from all the guests—out travelling on the cake." The writer recommends a snuffer, with which each child in turn could put out one candle. "I hear you say, 'Strange! I never thought of that before.'" And so the book proceeds through the rest of life—shake hands with clean gloves on (if you *must* shake hands), never let anyone pick up your handkerchief (never let anyone *see* your handkerchief)—reticulating a chain mail of rules that would both repress, conceal, cancel out a good half of bodily life, and at the same time stiffen, reassure, protect against all external and internal reproach the mind and spirit that observed them all. Developed in such detail and with such inflexible conviction, it becomes a *spiritual* discipline.

19

What is more surprising, at first reading, is the kind of class consciousness that permeates the whole system. There are rules given about introductions and wearing gloves and letters of thanks, but the book claims to be, and on the whole is, different from other etiquette manuals in that it assumes no social standing and no inherited manners in its readers. It warns you not to spit on other people's clothes, and not to twirl another person's beads while standing talking to her. It is aimed at the "business girl" from the poor immigrant home, and the kind of social event envisaged is the purely domestic dinner or small evening party. And yet, even in the most hygienic matters, you gradually realize, the sanction against doing the wrong thing is that it will expose you to the low opinion of "people who know." Certain acts class you with "the ordinaries," "the countrified," and "the vulgars." You will not be accepted among "nice people," "dainty people," "people of refined taste," or "people who know how things should be done." This sort of class feeling is strong in America, one realizes, much stronger than in England; a U and non-U division much lower down the social and intellectual scale, of which the signs are these iron rituals of hygiene and table manners, with none of the whimsey and wit of the British equivalent.

For one of the most interesting things is the way such an intense and elaborate insistence on correctness and even admission to an elite is so grandly indifferent not only to literary and artistic interests but to the kind of sensibility they foster. European arbiters of elegance, however stupid, would not dare *seem* so indifferent to all questions of tone, indirection, flexibility, originality. Above all, the insensitiveness to the absurd (the chapter on "The Sense of Humor" advises one to curb it) is of a kind every European will recognize as especially American. It is in this sense that one can set up that opposition between Refinement and Culture, and understand a little better what *The Europeans* is all about.

As for the femininity of it, the book's prescriptions are really practiceable perhaps only by the spinster, then, to some extent, by the childless wife, then by the mother with a maid, and so on down to that wretched adolescent boy. *"Men offend as frequently as women,"* it tells us in italics, though, "Some men think that manners are for women only." And in the chapter "Personality" there is a section headed "Men, Aren't You Funny?" which sufficiently indicates man's role in the world of manners. "Suppose that we women went through the streets singing at the top of our lungs! Imagine a woman, walking the street—say at ten o'clock at night—whistling so that you could hear her blocks away! Well, that is what you men do."

It is only in this book that I have found any serious expression of that destructive dominance of the American woman which one has often enough been assured of, and the effects of which one does seem to see in restaurants and bars. A little earlier in the same chapter there is a series of trenchant questions and comments that I can't end this piece better than by quoting.

Do you suppose that a girl likes to go out with you when you have a cigar between your teeth? Does she enjoy having you talk to her with a cigarette in your mouth? . . .

Is Alberta proud of you when you blow your nose so disgustingly loud that it sounds like the ugly snort of a huge ocean steamer?

Does she enjoy watching you hold your fork as a farmer holds a crowbar?

Doesn't she know that you have had no training when you hold a whole slice of bread in the palm of the hand and spread it with butter?

Isn't she embarrassed when you pile peas, potatoes, or any other food on the blade of a knife and so convey it to the mouth?

Perhaps some are thinking that a young man who would eat with his knife would be out with a girl who eats the same way. That is not necessarily true. Girls, I am sorry to say, are so anxious to go out and be entertained that they often accept invitations from inferior young men, hoping later, if they marry, to correct these crudities. The courtship is anything but pleasant, because the girl is constantly annoyed, but she does not mention the matter at that time for fear of "spoiling everything."

Much trouble later in life would be obviated if a girl had not

21

this fear; but since she has, one way of correcting the ultimate difficulty after marriage is reasonable tolerance on the part of the husband with the wife's commendable desire to improve the manners and speech of the one with whom she has cast her lot and who has promised to do everything to make her happy.

Remember, young man, when a girl corrects your manners, your speech, or criticizes your appearance, it is because she is grieved when you put yourself in the position to be ridiculed. A wife, if she is truly devoted to her husband, wants to shield him from unkind comment. One proof of her love is her criticism; and only a short-sighted, self-satisfied husband would resent it.

This book was first published in 1932, but a new edition came out in 1956, and there have been two reprints of that last edition, in 1956 and 1957.

I was lucky enough to get that first article accepted by a little magazine that specialized in Anglo-American cultural relations, and it appeared in spring, 1956, while I was in Turkey. I had not found a job the summer I was home, 1955; and I had found England deeply irritating and depressing; it made me feel again that my dissatisfactions were a sign of something wrong with me not with it. So in late August I took a post at a Turkish secondary school. Islam, however, did not seem to be the way out, and I spent a good deal of time brooding over the same question. Not purposively, of course; hardly consciously; just feeling dissatisfied with every conventional formulation; but sufficiently, in the end, for something to crystallize into this next piece.

The circumstances of that year account for many of its features. There were three of us English teachers isolated in a Turkish city, we were semiofficially sponsored by the British Council, we had a good deal to do with the Embassy in Ankara, a weekly copy of the Sunday Times was our only periodical reading—in sum, it was the official England, England's face for other countries, that I was shown.

The tone of this piece is still amusingly wobbly and "spirited," but the insights seem to me much clearer and come together to form a pattern. I have altered very little, and have *not tried to circumvent the objection I most commonly meet—and this applies to the first piece even more—that I have compared disparate things in the two countries. It seems to me that this is true only where I was not following an insight, but as it were restraining one, trying, in a justice-loving way, to be balanced and impartial, as in the two last sections of the preceding piece, where the femininity of American culture is on such a lower social and intellectual level than the British femininity to which it is compared. The British form of femininity now seems to me much the more sinister; both because the American with any vigor of mind dismisses this croaking phantom at the threshold of his life, if he ever entertained it, and because the thing I call femininity in England is so much more pervasive and shapeless, is better called a lack of masculinity. This is typical of the modifications of opinion I might now make; the effect of them all would be to sharpen, not to moderate, the challenge of the contrast.*

In another kind of case, where, to take perhaps the most extreme instance, I put Prince Philip and Princess Margaret side by side with Cary Grant and Grace Kelly, I would claim that the figures, to compare at all, must be disparate, because each is to be representative of his culture, and the cultures are disparate. Diana Dors, let us say, does not stand in the same relation to England as Marilyn Monroe does to America; she is, in the context of England, much more eccentric and dismissible. We cannot feel as warmly, in a public, national way, about such a personality; we need someone much more discreet and delicate, like, say, Moira Shearer. And when we can get that feeling with no commercialism at all, as with Princess Margaret, we are able to become really enthusiastic. These conditions, that we "cannot feel" something, and that we "need" something else, are the crucial facts. The notably similar figures in the two cultures (even when they do not just stand for "Britishness" in

America, or "Americanism" in England) are not the comparable ones because they stand in differing relation to their respective total configurations. Those configurations, and the perspective into which they put various human gestures, achievements, modes of being, are most centrally what I am trying to define, are America and England, from the point of view of these essays.

THOUGHTS ABOUT
TWO HOMES FROM ABROAD

Situated as I am, so far from both England and America, and equally close to each in loyalty, I keep putting them side by side in my mind. What keeps issuing from the comparison is a sense of something wrong with England. All England seems to speak with one too recognizable voice, about internal and external politics, about the theater and the cinema, about literature and music, about religion and morals; and it is, essentially, a dead voice. That is what I keep saying to myself. That word "dead," of course, requires a great deal of definition—or rather requires a definition of life, which I would hesitate to equate with America. But so many contrasts, so many details about both countries, fit together significantly—in the end, you feel sure, they all do—that some kind of pattern must emerge, wherever one begins.

The English Voice

What can "dead" mean, in this application? Well, the sensation that demands that name has announced itself often while one was reading the Sunday *Times;* the *Times's* kind of discretion, for one thing. When Glubb Pasha and the British officers in the Arab Legion were dismissed, the Sunday *Times* wrote this:

To a British public long accustomed to think of General Glubb not only as the creator of the Arab Legion but as one who has devoted his life to the welfare of the Trans-Jordanian Arabs, the shock of his summary dismissal will be equalled by the astonishment felt at the nation-wide demonstrations of joy which the news of his departure has evoked in Jordan. To close observers of Middle Eastern affairs, however, this evidence of "The Pasha's" unpopularity is not altogether unexpected, although the brutal ingratitude with which his services have been terminated is difficult to understand.

Equally difficult is it to assess the exact extent to which his influence in affairs of State was exerted, or to what degree, if at all, he assumed Ministerial powers.

The fact remains that, rightly or wrongly, it was popularly believed that the selection of Prime Ministers and their Cabinets, to say nothing of minor Governmental appointments, depended upon the grace and favour of "The Pasha." (March 4, 1956)

I wonder how large a British public thought about Glubb Pasha at all. It seems to me that he had been kept pretty quiet by those who knew; the only reaction to the name my education had given me was "a latter-day Lawrence of Arabia," a romantic, adventurous liberator-figure, Sir Walter Raleigh with a touch of Garibaldi; nothing more precise or realistic than that. As for "one who had devoted his life to the welfare of the Trans-Jordanian Arab," no one *thinks* in such terms at all. This is quite blatantly the language of nonthinking, of unrealism, of self-congratulation and self-consolation, of delusion. "The brutal ingratitude" of Glubb's dismissal seems to me comparatively easy to understand when the vital facts slip out in the next sentence or two. For surely those are vital facts, to the understanding not only of this event, but of the whole situation in the Middle East. To me, at least, it was an illumination to read that Jordan "depends for its very existence upon the subsidies it receives from the British Treasury," and that General Glubb commanded both the Arab Legion and the Jordanian police. It becomes clear that he had at his disposal far more than ministerial powers. Where is the difficulty in understanding the abolition of such an institution, in our day especially? Its existence seems much more bizarre to me. Its existence unacknowledged under our very noses seems to me almost criminal. Yet when we are told about it, it is (1) in this pompous, prize-day style—"equally difficult is it to assess"—and (2) after the event. This too is typical of the British attitude to public affairs. Once a thing has become history, it is allowed to have color and personality, even some spice. British history is full of romance; kings had mistresses and bartered away a colony for a kiss; prime ministers, even under Victoria, panted to be received in the best society, and would do anything for a duchess. But who decides, and how and why, contemporary problems, our problems— how many red-brick universities we should have, and what kind of men we get as M.P.s? This kind of inquiry is always answered with a short guide to parliamentary procedure and the party system. Whatever is contemporary is merely correct; though one knows that as soon as it becomes history one will be told that it was magnificently muddled, maliciously colorful, half-dictated by personality conflicts, and that all this will be quite complacently presented, as "in the inimitable British manner."

No American newspaper could blend, I think, that degree of intelligence and responsibility with that degree of stupidity and, in the long run, irresponsibility. There is some honesty and objectivity in the *Times* statement, as well as some real dignity, which, seen against the background of ordinary journalism, give the passage an impressiveness and significance; the impressiveness of a ceremonial and stately half-truth, which forbids the intrusion of the other half of the relevant thoughts by its virtues as much as by its defects. And if an American newspaper *should* blend the two in this way, it would not be so significant; first because no American paper has the power or representativeness of its British equivalent, and second because American papers differ so much more from each other, and even within their own pages. There are the independent news commentators and columnists, from Walter Lippmann and the Alsops down, to counterbalance the effects of the editorials. So there can never be this quiet assurance and unity of tone, nor consequently this deadness.

Two weeks later the leading article dealt with Cyprus.

The three-legged plan put forward by the Archbishop of Canterbury deserves most careful study, coming from so wise a leader of the Church, and in the course of a speech which had revealed Archbishop Makarios in his true light, self-condemned; behind the vestments of a prelate the calculations of a politician. . . . Finally, the Archbishop of Canterbury pleaded that Archbishop Makarios should be informed that his exile would end as soon as public order had been restored in Cyprus and that negotiations with him would be resumed as soon as the Constitution had been drafted. This plea is tempting but deceptive.

It involves several assumptions. The first is that as soon as "public order had been restored," and the exile brought back, terrorism would have ended for good. Past events offer no assurance whatever of this. If Archbishop Makarios, however, really repents, and is prepared consistently to oppose terrorism and disorder, a new situation will arise.

"So wise a leader of the Church," as a phrase, parallels "Her Majesty's interest in youth" or literature or slum-clearance. In serious discussion such elaborate politeness is out of place. And when Archbishop Makarios is revealed in his true light, what do we see? Behind the vestments of the prelate the calculations of the politician. The politeness is most naturally allied with a cloying elegance of style and a hopeless unrealism of thought. The most certified and acceptable history, the history I was taught in school, accepts, praises, *canonizes* prelates with political calculations. "Self-condemned" applies itself to the writing, not the subject. But above all it is the last sentence which seems to me so striking, both in itself and as an echo of the earlier article. If the Archbishop really repents, and is prepared consistently, etc., a new situation will arise. This is the tone of a schoolmaster (and a notably stupid and self-righteous one) to a boy, an inferior, one to be scolded and molded into one's own likeness. But the Cyprus question is politics, and our moral position is not so very superior as all that. It is hardly the moment to speak of really repenting, and promising never to do it again, in which case we might, just might, be prepared to think about forgiving. But the Sunday *Times* speaks to the world like a senior master to a school, of which the British government is headmaster. It expects from Jordan "gratitude," and from Cyprus "real repentance."

Authority, one might object, always does wrap itself in an impenetrable mystery of rectitude; but this is a newspaper talking, the fourth estate, the voice of discussion. This is comment and criticism. The truth is that in England the two are much alike—the tone of serious discussion and the voice of authority defending itself. I say tone and voice deliberately. One allows the Sunday *Times* full right to its opinion; what one objects to is its way of presenting that opinion, which in effect precludes discussion, and indicates that its own preliminary consideration has been limited and rigid. And the climate of opinion in England as a whole offers no resistance to, or control of, this; at a lower intellectual level the *Daily Express* blends authority with discussion in the same way, and the papers of the left, the *Daily Herald* and the *New Statesman,* are just as limited and rigid in their way of forming and presenting an opinion. There is no voice, and apparently no ear, for vigorous, flexible, autonomous discussion and criticism. Of course, there is such a thing as disagreement, about any subject discussed, but there is one complex of culture underlying and modifying both opinions. The literature-history-music half of the *New Statesman* is indistinguishable from that of the Sunday *Times* and the *Observer.* Culturally, everyone in England is a conservative; consequently, no debate goes really deep; it is conducted by both sides in this same voice that has never questioned itself really radically. There is one sensibility, one imagination, one set of sympathies and limitations of sympathy, in every mind, and they frame, shape, interpret every opinion, however radical-sounding. "Sell all your goods and give to the poor," delivered in an Oxford accent, becomes a perfectly conservative idea. Whatever the statement, promise, or criticism, the voice modifies it.

The Owner of That Voice

And to whom does this voice belong, most truly, most typically? To that old comic figure, the English gentleman. That is the real broadening of the mind that travel brings, which is, as so often, a salutary narrowing; to hear foreigners give you their outdated ideas of England, to laugh at them, and then to realize that they are still truer than one's own. Those human clichés, that have been laughed out of existence in England, still operate. It was their comic value that was laughed out of existence. They live on, disguised, superficially, by new opinions and an ironic awareness. One habitually hears the most violent, and often the most acute, criticisms of the gentlemanly mind, from people whose every positive, instinctive motion is purely in that tradition. If they are at all intelligent, the front of their minds must be nongentlemanly; but if their sources of life are not, also, this is merely a disguise. Being abroad helps you again; in the embassies they aren't at all disguised. There you meet gentlemen in the old style, such as Evelyn Waugh or Bernard Shaw might have created. At the British Council, the lecturers and librarians are privately, in personal conversation, as aware of contemporary facts as people at home; but they publicly present, and secretly dream of, the outdated official version of England without scruple, with the feeling that the facts are merely unfortunate, merely grimmer and more sordid than the myth. For the Welfare State is no gentleman's country, and an educated Englishman, whatever he may think about it, cannot feel it to be anything but unpalatable, or at best unexciting. And though their equivalents in England, in the Arts Council, the BBC, the stage, the universities, the professions, must live more in the present, is there one for whom the *ideal* life would not be to continue forever as an undergraduate at

Oxford or Cambridge? The facts of life in England in the twentieth century—every new novel attests it—either distress or bore every man of sensibility and discrimination in the country. And yet more people have better health, more money, better education, etc., etc., than ever before. But it is no longer a gentleman's country, and all the men of sensibility are gentlemen.

Of course, this is not a matter of the old outward manifestations of social difference. Times have changed and these—I mean the writers, actors, teachers, doctors—are people of intelligence and character. Those of them who would have been members of the ruling class fifty years ago, by right of birth, don't now rely on servants, Latin tags, or genealogical guarantee. And those who fifty years ago would have been untouchable, unreachable, are now completely accepted and assimilated. But it remains a class for all that, a group of people united by something much more subtle and powerful than economic interests or intellectual abilities. A university education is now becoming more indispensable than a public school one, it is true; and the average of academic intelligence among "gentlemen" must in fact be higher, but that makes little difference. This is no technocracy or intellectual elite. It is a social class, because it is bound together primarily by a community of tastes and habits in everything from religion to humor; very vague about religion, of course, but very definite about humor. There is a certain territory of mind which everybody has in common, where they all follow certain paths and honor certain mountains. For a map we may take the Sunday *Times* again, though there are many just as good. The religious piece is obviously written for a much less alert mind than Atticus or George Schwartz or E. H. Brooks and Son. In Russia, I presume, the doctrinal pieces are just as stringent as anything else. But the whole thing here, from Dilys Powell to Ernestine Carter, has this unity of tone. When a new writer comes along, like Roger Bannister or Siriol Hugh Jones, he is exactly like the ones he succeeds. That unity is not, like *The New Yorker's* tone, mostly

32

metropolitan. The Sunday *Times* is much more official and broadly based, much more the voice of England, not London. Obviously there is much of America to which *The New Yorker* is alien. But the only thing that could alienate an educated man from the Sunday *Times* is a difference of politics. Because every educated man in England is a gentleman.

With all the equalizing regulations of the Welfare State, England remains one of the most class-conscious countries in the world; and labor-management relations are no better than in the days when one could blame the inherent hostility of capitalist and proletarian; because the new managers are just as "ruling class" as the old. They assume involuntarily a superiority which is not only that necessary to responsibility, but that of the whole mind. It is fashionable now to call it a difference, but it amounts to a superiority when the hostility must always be condescending from one side and aggressive from the other. And you need only think of America to realize that far more savage conflicts of economic interest can result in far less class feeling.

Of course, there are class distinctions in America. Even, most obviously in the East, there is class feeling. But the figure of the Ivy League graduate, which best corresponds to the gentleman in England, is not clear enough, pervasive enough, or powerful enough, to attract the resentment of Pittsburgh miners, or Midwestern farmers, to be in any dramatic relationship to them. It is in relation to other college graduates, and to purely social life for people between eighteen and twenty-eight in the big cities, but that is all. It does not stand for the country as a whole, or for the ruling class as a whole in relation to the rest of the country. America is not dominated by any single type, much less this class-limited one, and so does not suffer, as England does, from this type of oppressive uniformity.

The Anesthetic Effects of This Voice

Moreover, to pass to more personal areas, this tyranny of the one mind in England seems to affect, to blight, not only the

33

tastes and habits one acquires, but the enthusiasm with which one holds them. By its emphasis on elegance, understatement, lightness of touch, it makes everything less vivid, less valuable, for us as we're growing up. As minds go, of course, this one has its virtues, though even of those we have had enough. The humor, the discretion, the good manners, the sense of continuity, the sense of public responsibility, they all rather irritate now. But more insistent are its vices: the lack of personal adventure, the lack of inner life, the unwillingness to take great things greatly. We are, as a nation, turned outward, away from the inner life; and we don't recognize it, because it isn't to great possessions, but to cultural stewardship and propriety, that we turn. Of course, there is plenty of impropriety and plenty of personal adventure; impudent, mischievous, even humorous; of the kind Evelyn Waugh describes. But self-respecting, self-propagating, passionate life—where will you find that? This makes an inner deadness which the growing mind may not recognize, being the only thing that mind is used to, but which operates nevertheless as a sterilizer of the world, making harmless everything that might, through excess of life, threaten conformity. So much is reduced to a diversion; drama to elegant performances; art to the Old Masters; so much to a decorum— politics and history presented as the celebration and evolution of the *status quo*. I well remember my own awakening at eighteen, when I was taught by a man who felt what I afterward gradually realized to be a passion for what he believed in. I had to invent the word for myself to fit the phenomenon.

A priori and a posteriori, America does not suffer from this kind of blight.

The Two Countries Face to Face

One would like to contrast America with England in some wholesale way at this point, but it is very difficult, precisely because there is not one mind or one voice in America. There is a residual agreement and similarity, of course, between *The New Yorker* and the *Kenyon Review* and the Actors Studio, but that is not the same thing. There is the American Way of Life, of course, but that's below the Plimsoll line of serious thinking, while Britishness isn't. Where is the Sunday *Times* of America, the map of the American mind? It does not exist. The American mind in that tyrannizing, limiting sense does not exist. This is why the American graduate is apt to feel a kind of inferiority in the presence of an Englishman. It is not that the latter knows more, but he seems to have a more general knowledge, he understands more that he has not studied, he knows how to treat serious things lightly, upon occasion, and light things seriously; he moves easily and independently in the world of the mind. Why? Because he has a map, a contour map even, showing heights and depths. Or, more exactly, because he knows everyone else to have the map, and so does not regale fellow travelers with the obvious. He does not think he has discovered things for the first time.

The graduate of an American state university, on the other hand, is likely to think he knows only those subjects in which he has taken a course. Any less documented and demonstrated knowledge is likely to seem to him too flimsy to be taken seriously. The world of knowledge, humanities, sciences, arts stretches away from him in all directions, without known limits; he feels he could go on learning all his life, and at the end of that time, on his last day, discover the highest mountain of all. This is just one example of that sense of endless development, of process, which many observers have pointed out as the trait which distinguishes the American mind from anything European. The Americans have no sense, comparatively, of predetermined limits, of necessary form. They don't feel, for instance, as most Europeans do, that human nature is so limited that democracy can be only an ideal. And because they don't feel in this way, they make democracy work, just as because they don't think human knowledge is already charted out, they really discover truths. They *are*, comparatively, unlimited; in the same sense that the physical U.S.A. is unlimited, unformed, by comparison with England, France, or Germany.

35

There is one thing, however, in the American environment which all Americans have in common, and that is the very variety of it. To an Englishman the human geography of America is as fantastic and improbable as the physical. Cities like Phenix City, Alabama, for instance, localities like the Tennessee mountain villages, religious sects (even one so enlightened as the Dutch Reformed Church), all these are without parallel in England. Crime, vice, poverty, riches, purity, prejudice, dedication, all find expression of an energy which we have only read about, in history books, which we have never known as our contemporary reality, which our minds are not really ready to accept. We tend to think, we feel, that the twentieth century, or civilization at least, has outgrown that sort of thing. And consequently there is in the Americans, as contrasted with us, a sort of weather-beaten quality, from having been more exposed to sharper extremes of climate, which corresponds somewhat to the bluff, open-air effect they achieve at the hairdresser's and under the sun lamp. We are drawing-room creatures by comparison. I think that helps to explain how we can achieve so many kinds of artificiality, of manner, style, accent, opinion, conduct; how we can so loftily patronize them.

Going to America with a bunch of Fulbright scholars from England was quite an experience. The entire crossing was one gesture on their part, which they planned to continue over the year, of unhesitating, unqualified patronage of America. There were sixty or seventy of them, both men and women, anywhere between twenty and thirty, students in every subject and from every part of the country, but all had an air of gilded youth about them, triumphantly unrelated to their personal incomes, and in despite of their actual eagerness for "something for nothing." It was the genuine Oxford and Cambridge gilt, for all that, the sense of privilege, the sense of responsibility, though a responsibility in this case mainly to *épater le bourgeois*. They had such a sense of style, overriding everything else, that they felt the true test of education was the ability to talk brilliantly about nothing. They had such a sense of community, of alliance that, seeing a friend in a crowd, they called out to him, not oblivious of, but triumphant over, the hundred other faces that turn to observe—the hundred outsiders. They were going to America essentially to see with their own eyes the huge improbabilities they knew were there; they saw it as an immensely extended version of Hearst's San Simeon, half treasure house, half Hall of Mirth; they came planning anecdotes for when they returned. Never did they expect to learn anything useful or interesting to themselves as educated people trying to lead a civilized life. They would have if they had been going to France. If they had been going to India, even, they would have had a sense of the differentness, the possible partial superiority of what they were going to see. They would have had something approximating to a readiness for reverence. But not in America; they knew the vast cultural vacuum they would find there. And they would find it! Listening to the best orchestra, they would see the banality or the eccentricity of the program, the banality and eccentricity of the audience. Americans in England sometimes do the same. But sometimes they put it all down to our credit. Both possibilities are open to them, and so sometimes, a little more often than we, they arrive at a just estimate. They are relatively unprejudiced.

Whereas the English educated man, the modern English gentleman, is made hostile to America, as he is hostile to democracy and contemporaneity and normality, by the essence of his education. The English university, after all, is a hothouse. Its pride and joy is the exotic, the eccentric, the man radically different from the man in the street. Even the average undergraduate is encouraged to acquire affectations and become unordinary. And so any lowering of the temperature, however slight, however normal and healthy, is apt to seem a change for the worse. The metaphor is apt, I think, because the English university is so much a matter of temperature and humidity, of climate. I mean that it is a social institution, with a social mission; it transmits a heritage of wisdom, not of learning; whatever they are studying, the students are more keenly learning what tone of voice to use for Hollywood, which attitudes are permissible toward sex, how to be brilliant in conversation. How to be brilliant more than how to make sense; brilliance means not knowing things other people know as much as it means knowing things they don't, not working for an exam as much as doing well in it. It usually connotes some lack of interest in, incapacity for, ordinary life. Of course, the average undergraduate knows that in three or four years after leaving the university he will have shed all the exaggeration and will be a discreet, humorous, above all things moderate, gentleman. This was all a part of his formation. But his private tastes, his sensibility, continue to point and vibrate in the direction the university gave them. He stays essentially anti-American.

The Two Countries Facing the Future

This scheme of development, this kind of personality, are of course in essence quite compatible with the keenest intelligence, the greatest vigor, the deepest satisfaction. But they have today become clichés; today only stupid people can use their phrases without irony; intelligent people, if they share their feelings, are condemned to self-deprecation. Above all, these characteristics, this manner, are now unreasonable and unseasonable, out of all relation to every contemporary or future reality. It is an aristocratic manner. And our only future is democratic.

I sometimes think people don't realize that enough. Whatever our personal aptitudes or preferences, whatever society we would build if we had a choice, we are committed to democracy. Our fathers and grandfathers committed us. It is natural to rebel at the moment we realize we are committed to the banal; we all know the absurdities and indignities of democracy, we could all be brilliant reactionaries; but nature also demands that we quickly accept what is necessary. We have got to learn how to make real democracy work, with all its disadvantages. There is no other decent future. This real democracy is not a matter of more votes or more trade unions. The task ahead is to create a democratic mind, in which the assent and interest of the millions are gained for the work of the few, the creation of beauty, the achievement of life. Hitherto the interest of the millions has been available only to projects for more money, more food, more films, or war. Most of the great achievements of civilization, particularly contemporary ones, have left the millions indifferent or hostile. In America—in England too—there is a real, self-righteous hostility to distinction of mind or manner, to intensity of thought or feeling, to criticism, to many kinds of greatness. Our formidable spread of education in the last fifty years has probably increased that hostility more than it has created understanding. If a democratic mind is to be born, the hierarchy of values will have to be maintained and fed from sources different from those of the past. For that, after all, is the basic problem, the transmission of the knowledge of the few down to the many quickly enough for society to remain vitally homogeneous. One man, let us say, can read Dante and understand his peculiar significance for this generation; ten men know enough to distinguish his work from that of others who claim the same. Fifty men are sure about the ten, and can understand what they point out; a thousand men—and so on. The great work of a society's mind is to ensure that knowledge and influence follow these channels and not others. This happens well enough in science today. We have, even many of us who are highly educated people, not the remotest idea of why Einstein is right, or what modern physics is about, but we know that he is right. We know that he is a brilliant scientist, that he deserves our respect, that the people who are presented to us as scientists really are what they claim to be, and so on. All without the slightest personal check. And not only us, but the man in the street too. That is as it should be. What a different story in the arts. But it has happened there, in the past. In nineteenth-century England everybody who read, however philistine, knew that Tennyson and Browning were great poets, and that great poets were great men. They knew in the same way that we know about science today. But the actual machinery by which the knowledge was transmitted will not do for us today, because it was not democratic. Gentlemen recognized another gentleman and knew how far to trust him; literature and publicity limited themselves instinctively to the gentlemanly. Nowadays we have other truths, other types, other means of communication; gentlemanliness is a luxury, not a necessity, a self-deprecating archaism, not a natural part of life. Therefore what we need is a body of men, both fully democratic, unaristocratic in sensibility, and still fully convinced of the values of the few, in key cultural positions, who might there form a sort of heart, a central ganglion of that mind. These men, if any, will make democracy possible. Where shall we find them?

In England, the only possibility attests the impossibility. Kingsley Amis's heroes are both highly intelligent, essentially educated men, and at the same time fully committed to democracy, democracy of feeling as well as of elections; deeply and intimately aware of how education in England unfits one for the function I have been describing. But they are isolated rebels; the storm of protest that greeted *Lucky Jim* proves how much they are the exceptions that prove the rule. Moreover, they find their problem insoluble, their situation untenable. The author provides them with merely personal, if not wish-fulfillment, salvations. Jim Dixon is caught up into his *machina* by an art-loving millionaire *deus,* and whisked away out of mortal view. John Lewis goes back to The People. There is no real solution. They are doomed to defeat socially.

In America? In America, it seems to me, one meets people who combine a simplicity and solidity of temperament with a genuinely adventurous mind, and sufficient shrewdness and self-confidence to keep them from disaster. And one finds them in the sort of place where they can do most good—teaching Freshman English Composition at the universities, for instance. At their best their keynote is a sort of determined ambition, a half-amused realization of being out on a limb, perilously separated from the mass. They have, in their personal and group past, all the huge unredeemed populace. Their ambition for the future has been, until they met it, education, culture, gentlemanliness. Now, as a satisfactory present and future, they have only each other, only more isolated fragments. It is up to them to make a new world; to explain and excuse to their parents and cousins and friends and pupils their differentness; to make the practical decisions that follow from their new insights, the votes, the agitations, the sympathies and apathies, palatable and influential in their communities. They are characterized, often, by domesticity and financial struggles. And financial struggles, especially in America, make it particularly necessary and difficult to explain oneself. They cannot say, as their equivalent in England can, though tacitly of course, "I have risen in the world, I enjoy the company, putatively, of power and wealth." They can hardly say, "It is because I love my fellow man"; so much of the change in them is toward criticizing their fellow, common, man. They must explain, somehow, that there are other values, and they are living for them. Their life is privately, inherently, as well as publicly, professionally, a reconciliation of the contented, self-respecting life of the many with the dissatisfactions of the few. If men like these can teach in the junior colleges and English Composition courses, review for newspapers and magazines, produce in the repertory theaters, etc., something like the hierarchy of values may be maintained and the democratic mind may be born. If they can, for instance, persuade students to read *The Catcher in the Rye,* to overcome their distrust of Holden Caulfield, to sympathize, to the extent necessary to understand the book, with his rebellion, then they will have quite notably stretched their minds, enriched their sympathies, educated them, given them a share in the mind of their nation.

In England, obviously, there is no parallel social group, and it seems to me that nobody performs a parallel function. No one spends his middle twenties, from twenty-three to twenty-seven, say, explaining the intellectual life to a mass of disinterested eighteen-year-olds who represent a more or less average intelligence. Thirty per cent of the age group in America go to college and take Freshman English, but it would be misleading to say the top 30 per cent. The minds of most students in a big state university are so completely undeveloped, untrained to deal with the kind of general problem Freshman English presents, that the teacher in fact deals with the "American mind." I mean the student is so innocent of the often snobbish discriminations, cynicisms, knowingnesses, which every European university student acquires in high school, that even the really intelligent repeat the most blatant magazine clichés and raise the most outrageous objections to the very act of criticism, with complete sincerity and considerable energy. The teacher has to answer the simplest questions, the simplest objections to his whole value system, and the simplest questions are always the hardest; he has to dramatize his answers, enact them, be in front of the class something they can recognize as valuable as well as critical, human as well as intellectual. No one has to do that in England, especially at that period of his life. That 30 per cent of the population in England don't get the intellectual life explained to them. Above all, the real elite never go through that testing, make that contact. The bright young men who go into the BBC, the British Council, the Arts Council, after Oxford and Cambridge, never have to defend themselves; rarely do they defend their values, their stock-in-trade, be it modern painting, ancient music, or English literature; essentially their job is to fight for those things, to grab space and time and opportunity of performance for them away from inferior and rival alternatives. Their job too is education, but it takes the essential act and the early stages for granted, and works on the refinements; if they—and it is rare—work at raising the level of general thinking or entertainment, it is in a repressive, uplifting, governessy way, from outside, not inside.

I choose these examples for comparison because it is at that level that the gap is most disastrous, the connections most frail, in both countries. We have men of learning at the universities, we have men of talent writing poetry and music, but at the moment it is not from them that even any considerable leavening of the mass of the people draw their ideas in England or America, but from popular oracles largely hostile to the forms of contemporary sensibility. What we have in England is the old aristocratic machinery (the sense of community the vicar, the doctor, the J.P., the squire in the village all shared, the common cultural responsibility) as an apparatus for conducting the best ideas down to a socially effective level; and this is now very elaborately adapted to modern conditions, by the multitude of scholarships, by BBC television, by life peerages for men of distinction, by the Welfare State. But the machinery remains aristocratic, and so basically inadequate; the really new, really vital things cannot make use of it, are at war with it, just because of their vitality; so that in effect it can pass on only the harmless.

Historically America has lacked all such machinery; nowadays it is still discrete, and a mess, but in the mess it seems to me there are some people—emerging or submerging, I don't know—who could become, as I said, the heart, the mind, of a democracy. In them there is the glimpse of a tolerable future. In them one can feel a steadiness and passionateness—provoked by the rawer realities of American life—which simply do not exist in England. In them one can see a world and a group to which one can want to belong.

One cannot say, psychologically any more than metaphysically, that one wishes one were an American, because the one that wishes is an irredeemably British thing; it would be the same as wishing the annihilation of the image of oneself; it is only that if it were possible to get a prenatal mid-Atlantic opportunity to choose, I think it is westward most people would likely choose to go.

That is it, then. England is suffocating in the grip of a class, no less than fifty years ago; more, because that class's vitalities have failed and receded, and so its limiting, characterizing traits now weigh more heavily, more deadly. Moreover, this class is originally, ineradicably, undemocratic. In these two ways America, which we despise, stands for health, and we stand for sickness. Our hostility to America is both symptom and quite deadly infection. And there is much more chance, in America, of national life becoming something significant, something to command one's loyalties.

I had not been in Turkey very long before I decided that I must go back to America. I had left over a quarrel with the university about the dissertation I was writing. A demand for one more revision made me count up how much practical hypocrisy and formalism, how great an indignity, the Ph.D. process was forcing on me, and I withdrew fairly haughtily. But not finding a job in England, much less the reassurance of final return, of being among my own kind at last, had sapped my pride; and Turkey, interesting though it was, scarcely struck me as a possible home; above all, if it was now out of the question for me to live in England—I could not put it to myself so directly, of course, but neither could I avoid in some manner believing it—I was free to choose, almost hedonistically, any kind of exile that attracted me. I decided that writing a thesis under even the strictest direction went no more against my grain than drifting on from Konya to Aden to perhaps Hong Kong, teaching English conversation to foreigners. The things that mattered to me obviously could not be found in any life so much made up of observation, so little of participation. Teaching Freshman English in America was the form of exile that gave the most satisfaction to the ambitions, disappointments, resentments which the state of exile in itself aroused in me. Besides, as you can tell from the last piece, I was a good deal in love with America.

I suffered a certain disillusionment about that; the graduate school I returned to had fewer married war veterans, more careerist English majors with a taste for elegance; and some I had known before I now saw debilitated, dehydrated, even so filleted they could bend six ways at once, by the process of getting their Ph.D. But I did not change my mind about the group as a whole. I was only glad I had seen the good things when they were most unmistakable.

Other of my enthusiasms, for other parts of the American experience, revived even more strongly on return. The multifariousness, which from a distance seems so doomed to disappear, so much a thing of the past already, is after all a triumphantly effective force; in spite of all the machinery of normalization, the mass media and their incessant propaganda, with national styles in everything from haircuts to best-sellers, Americans from Georgia continue to differ from New Yorkers and from Midwesterners in vigorous and meaningful ways; since the forces that make for unity have intensified their powers so much in the last hundred years, and since variety continues to exist, it seems clear that there must be very tough powers of resistance, of differentiation, also at work. The physical splendor and opulence of the country, both in purely natural and in human forms, which from a distance can seem so irrelevant and accidental, are after all a continuing fact, a day-by-day source of excitement and satisfaction. The generosity, confidence, energy, availability of the people, which at a distance can so easily be dismissed as the result of an expanding economy, when you are there, have effects, not causes; however temporary, they are actual; and in fact they are given every guarantee of permanence, by being reflected in the culture's dominant images. These facts are simple, and well known; but defined abroad they sound more vulgar and feeble, above all more theoretical, than they are; only coming to America or, better, coming back, can do them justice.

Once re-established in Ann Arbor, I did not resume my train of thought about the two countries; I had no train of thought; I had merely made a series of observations. These were delivered, the subject was off my mind, and I was concerned with other ideas and other pieces of writing with a much greater sense of inspiration. When it was suggested to me that I should write something about the British Establishment, I was so far from pregnant with the subject that I thought the phrase referred to the Church of England. Set right, I looked around for something to say; I hoped at best to avoid repeating my last piece too blatantly or dully; and I found, to my surprise, that observations, comparisons, connections, generalizations, a whole stream of ideas gushed from some hidden source in my mind with a profusion and force and clarity I'd never before known. It was a little uncanny that this should have been so externally prompted; as if a stranger knew more about what one was thinking than one did oneself.

"BRITAIN" AND BRITAIN

I

The idea of an Englishman in most Americans' minds is something quite clear and vivid and single; he is polite, diffident, with a murmurous, richly cultured voice—whimsical and witty, though with a rigid, unspoken moral code—his hair is rather long and his clothes rather Edwardian, generally a suggestion of conscious fancy dress, but surprisingly sharp-witted and strong-willed underneath. Lord Peter Wimsey. Rex Harrison. Mr. Macmillan. And of course Englishmen are like that. Only it's a small minority of them. These are "Britishers."

It is not so easy to define and specify the merely British. The Northerner, for instance, who is still a type, a myth, at the level of popular jokes and music hall songs in England, has received no attention at the upper levels of culture for many years. The figure to compare and contrast in America is the Southerner. Characters in J. B. Priestley's books and his own public persona are versions of this Northern idea; I think those are the most intense apprehensions and presentations of the North in my lifetime. And yet it is possible to be, and great numbers of Englishmen are, most valuably intelligent and mature in a distinctively Northern way. The Northerner—that is, the man from Lancashire and Yorkshire—is tougher, blunter, dowdier, warmer than the Southerner; usually an industrial worker, always a proletarian, altogether less pretentious, less cosmopolitan, less socially flexible, more strongly rooted in himself and his own fireside. The one adequate symbol is Gracie Fields, the greatest British entertainer of our time. Her kind of humor, unsophisticated but keen-witted, her kind of charm, plain, honest, hearty, unseductive, her kind of energy, gawky rather than graceful, her piercingly direct and simple sentimentality, these are Lancashire personified. But other parts of the country produce British, not "British," types. Somerset, for instance, produced Ernest Bevin, the only politician I remember to reach cabinet rank without becoming "British" on the way. His roughness, heaviness, slowness, dowdiness, his obvious integrity, his self-declared limitedness were the direct antithesis of Anthony Eden. Photographs of him fox-trotting at Moscow with Lady Diana Duff-Cooper, or of Mrs. Bevin at a fashion show in Paris accompanied by Mrs. Churchill, were both ludicrous and immensely encouraging. Or take the industrial Midlands, Nottinghamshire and Derbyshire. And here, for the first and only time, we have the advantage that our subject has been seen for us and given to us by a brilliant sensibility. The home life of Paul and Miriam in *Sons and Lovers,* the first half of *The Lost Girl,* short stories by Lawrence like "Fanny and Annie" and "Tickets, Please" should convince us that there are many ways of being British, deeply exciting and admirable ones, related to the "British" way only by antithesis.

All the people I have mentioned are fully the product of their social situation, their England, and they are fully alive and important human beings. They are not, as the world assumes, half-finished products, halfway toward being "British." They have all, in fact, an implicit hostility to, and a need to attack, polish, brilliance, and dignity of that kind. *"La pudeur," "la froideur," "le phlegme anglais,"* those were the phrases I had thrown at me in France; no wonder the French consider Galsworthy and Charles Morgan better representatives of England than Lawrence. In America it is polish, culture, and an almost sinister Old World charm I feel people looking for in me, but the majority of British people don't specialize in those commodities.

Nowadays the North and all the other districts have disappeared from the map, the Northerner is only a comic, one-dimensional figure; in a film a local accent signalizes humorous relief —only characters speaking BBC English are to be taken seriously. In the past it was not always so. Mrs. Gaskell's *North and South* deals with the difficulties of adjustment for a girl from the South going to live in the North: the difference in landscape, language, economic mode, condition of the people, social life, manners and morals; a difference as dramatic as that between North and South in America. After 1800 it was, of course, the siting of the big factories and mines in the North which dominated the contrast. But there were differences before then. The Danes settled much more heavily in the North —the language still bears traces of it; William the Conqueror radically impoverished it in the effort to subordinate it when he regulated his new kingdom; all the early kings encouraged and protected the South, which was much more theirs, and merely ruled the North. For eight centuries the North lived to itself, played a very small part in British history. Chaucer, Shakespeare, Milton, Pope, Johnson, there are no great names that occur to one anywhere north of Warwickshire, north of the circle whose center was London and the monarchy and the artery to the Continent. England's second great port was Bristol. The cities of the North were York, Chester, Durham, administrative centers. Birmingham, Manchester, Leeds, Wolverhampton, Liverpool, Sheffield were villages. When they became great cities in the nineteenth century, they did take their place on the cultural map, but as a question mark, a Dark Continent, whose inhabitants, it was presumed, would be given a language and a form in due time. Mrs. Gaskell and Disraeli tackled the problem, but were not big enough for it; and no great writers took up their work. George Eliot belonged to the nonindustrial Midlands. The Brontes' genius was directed inward. Our great lower-middle-class writers, Dickens and Wells, belonged to the

South. There have never been any working-class writers in England. And during this century, of course, literature has retreated
up the social ladder. All our authors are public schoolboys—
Waugh, Greene, Auden, Isherwood, Connolly, even Orwell.
Public schoolboys cannot belong to any locality. They are
"British," gentlemen, ruling class. The bulk of the population,
after its one heave toward speech in the nineteenth century, has
sunk back into silence.

The one exception to this is again D. H. Lawrence. He is the
one writer of this century who is not "British"; he is the one
writer who has seen and taken seriously the British; he is the
one who has, or could have, given a voice to these other parts of
the population. And he is the exception who proves the rule.
Despite the amazing extensions of vision and technique he
introduced in the novel, no writer since has made use of them.
Think how many have used Henry James's techniques, and
Eliot's in poetry. The reason is that Lawrence was not "British";
his mind, his sensibility, his temperament, the essence of him
is alien to those who are. They cannot learn from him. This
same alienation is obvious in Orwell's ineffectual attempts to
feel like, be like, a working-class man.

It is also significant that so many great writers in English
this century have not been English by birth. Eliot, James, Conrad, Joyce, Yeats; how much of great vision is left when those
names are taken away? And all these naturally knew only the
educated aristocracy. They had no intimate understanding of
people like Lawrence's parents and friends. They could only
see them from a great distance, as underground creatures. Their
versions of England have always grouped the "British" in the
foreground, with a few worthy but comic retainers for relief.

II

But it would not be so important merely that the outside
world takes "Britain" for Britain. The dangerous thing is that
England does, too. It does not take Ernest Bevin or Gracie
Fields or D. H. Lawrence seriously, because they are not edu-

cated. That is why they seem half-finished products. Education in England is inseparable from the process of becoming "British." Let us say, to avoid the irritating quotation marks, becoming a gentleman. However much like Ernest Bevin or Gracie Fields your parents may be, you must become much more like Anthony Eden before you feel able to write a novel, or even to express a confident opinion about novels. All the modes of expression in the country are controlled by gentlemen; the world of the arts, of the universities, of the educated press, of the refined entertainments, of teaching, of administration, are all controlled by gentlemen. Their sensibility is dominant; there is no other sensibility. Before an Englishman feels ready to think—not merely to express himself—but to *think* about more than local matters, he must recast himself in that mold. More usually, he will find he has been so molded from the age of eleven.

For nowadays gentlemen are not, of course, those born into certain families or large incomes. I think that in no country in the world is the career so open to the talents as in England now. Gentlemen are in fact an intellectual aristocracy; and yet they remain at the same time essentially a social class. How this can be, the process by which the class is selected and trained, I may perhaps best illustrate by my own case. I was born into a lower-class family, none of whose members, on either side, had been even to secondary school, but at eleven I took an examination which every child in the country now takes, and was sent free to the county grammar school. Approximately the top 10 per cent in that examination go to the grammar school, and the yearly intake is divided into three classes, again on the principle of ability, so that the children I competed against during my school career were, theoretically, the brightest 3 per cent of my contemporaries. And we competed in a way that an American would scarcely imagine, perhaps. We got marks, not grades, out of twenty for an exercise or an essay, out of a hundred for an exam, and at the end of each term we were arranged in order, from first to thirtieth, in each subject, and again, all the marks being added together, from first to thirtieth in the form. All this is mostly pedagogy, of course, but it has its educational effect, too. It magnifies the intellectual process in our eyes, fosters a quick-witted apprehension and manipulation of facts, and a disrespectful familiarity with areas of knowledge and systems of thought; but above all, by thus isolating, stimulating, exposing our busy little minds, it makes us extraordinarily malleable, in our deepest imaginations, by the teacher.

The grammar school teacher in England is a very important person, much more so, both for the influence he has and for the tradition he represents, than the high school teacher in America. His level of intelligence and education is high, especially teachers in the arts subjects, who are often Oxford and Cambridge graduates; a good number of our writers, painters, musicians, thinkers have been grammar school teachers at the beginning of their careers. In America the same men would be university teachers. They more than anyone else in our lives represent to that top 10 per cent in the grammar schools the maturely intelligent man, give our minds their mildly, Britishly academic cast, set that stamp on the national type. The grammar school teacher is the key symbol of modern Britain, the modern John Bull, in his armchair, in a tweed sports coat, with leather-patched elbows, smoking and reading. He is shabbier, more resigned than the "Britisher" described before, but under the domination of the same idea—what he is *reading* is probably Evelyn Waugh or Dorothy Sayers. His great emblem is the pipe, with all its connotations of relaxed, shrewd, twinkling, masculine geniality; he has had and given up larger ambitions; he is the onlooker at life, very good at crossword puzzles, the piano, and carpentry; he knows a great deal. To the bright boy from a poor, uneducated home, he is the all-obliterating symbol of authoritative, intelligent manhood, impressed on his mind at its most malleable moment. His tones of voice, his jokes, his clothes, his reading, his opinions are the ones which for the boy, accept or reject them *personally* as he will, must remain emotionally charged with all the energy of the "correct thing."

A good example of the type, and the profound influence he exerts, is Mr. Holmes in Isherwood's *Lions and Shadows*. Mr. Holmes was a public school teacher, but the difference is not important. The state grammar schools are avowed imitations of the public schools. The majority of them were set up in consequence of the Education Act of 1911, when it must have seemed there was no better model. The house system, the prefect system, the emphasis on games, the idea of school spirit, all these are transplants from the public school. In one profound sense they are doomed to defeat, because they are not boarding schools, and the homes the children go back to each day have no sense of special privilege and responsibility, so the hothouse atmosphere necessary for a private social code is broken open and dissipated. So while the grammar school turns out gentlemen, they are in a depressed, deprecatory, slightly charlatan modern mode; because almost the primary fact in the consciousness of the staff and the bright boys is that they are not public schools, that most of the boys aren't what they are supposed to be—they have no idea of school spirit, for instance—and that even the thinkers themselves are not really real gentlemen. They deceive themselves, of course. They are gentlemen—in the modern mode.

One extracurricular activity deserves special mention, the debating club. Debates in English schools are over ordinary topics, like "Can any good come of war?" etc. What is extraordinary is the excess of formality and lack of reality. We begin, after all, at thirteen, long before the subjects could mean much to us, and before discussion, let alone debate, could be a natural activity. The same is true of our essays on "Humility, the Christian Virtue" at the same age. The aim is openly, exclusively, successfully, to sharpen our wits. Quite often, for example, we have frankly fantastic subjects like "That this house believes in Father Christmas," and they are argued just as acutely, just as elaborately, with the same formal, self-conscious politeness. These, in fact, are the really characteristic and really impressive

54

displays. This influence continues through the years at the university. The Oxford and Cambridge Unions are much the largest undergraduate organizations; the post of President of the Union is a very high recommendation in the outside world; and the emphasis is again on brilliant manipulation of the rules of debate, and of the essential paradox of the situation. For the situation is essentially make-believe, but must be taken seriously up to a point—and not beyond. This is the essence of "civilization" as the word is used in England. Mr. Colville, in his article in the October, 1957, issue of *Harper's Magazine,* mentions the precocious sophistication of English undergraduates. The debate is a good example of the influences that cause that sophistication; it is sophistry, in the full sense. To hear an Oxford debating team, especially before an American audience, is to appreciate something fantastic.

Finally let us mention the sixth form, the top class in every grammar school, composed of that 25 per cent of each year that stays on after getting their school certificates, to prepare for the university or some further training. The sixth (another legacy of the public school to the grammar school) is quite different from any other form in the school, and has a powerful mystique. Boys in the sixth are given many privileges, exempted from many rules, have their own library and study, free periods to work by themselves, and most of them become prefects, responsible for the discipline of the rest of the school; they are grown up (in official theory, of course); they become (again the practice is not exactly like the theory) the intellectual equals of the teachers, initiates of the port-wine, pipe-smoking, Latin-tagging society of the staff room. They are taught by the best teachers in the school, which means the Oxford and Cambridge graduates, the most genuine gentlemen. The classes are very small, as few as three and four. They are taken into the teachers' confidence, which does not mean, as it might here, that the teacher interests himself in the boy's private life; in England the movement is in the reverse direction, and the boy is allowed to hear the master's frankest comments on the events of the day, however cynical and amoral they may be. I was not yet fifteen when I entered the sixth, and I spent three years in that intellectual and spiritual forcing house. By eighteen I was a gentleman, beyond hope of reprieve.

I had been radically separated from my home and relations; not by any crude snobbery, but by a genuine and inevitable introduction into a new mental world, with all sorts of tastes and desires. I had slid over from Gracie Fields to Anthony Eden; there hadn't seemed to be any halfway mark. Of course, I wasn't the "Britisher" I described before. Nobody could be that flagrant, except abroad. I saw through Lord Peter Wimsey at sixteen. But I remained a subdued, self-conscious, negative variant of him, because it never occurred to me there was any other way to be for a sensitive, intelligent person. I echoed his sort of remarks about women and wine and nonconformists and the French, in a highly self-conscious, largely self-denying way, as if I weren't really saying them.

Most of the boys in the sixth go on to the universities (under 2 per cent of their age group), and their expenses, for living as well as fees, are completely paid by the state. I spent three years reading English at Cambridge, three years of a minimum of external, formal control, but under a much stricter formative pressure than I'd have known at an American university. Attendance at lectures was not checked, nor even much desired, nor did one write papers for the lecturer; I went once a week to a supervisor, who told me frankly he'd be better pleased if I would stay away, and wrote three or four essays a term for him, strictly when *I* felt like it, on *my* initiative. There were no grades. All one had to do was prepare for the final exams; copies of old papers were available; books were available in the libraries; and there was—we were always being reminded of it —all the brilliant conversation in the world. That was the freedom. On the other hand, we were very conscious of the limits of what it was possible to say or think or feel about everything important. As far as study was concerned, we had already been specializing heavily in English for three years. All that remained was more specialization. And the university's emphasis was much more on general education, on wisdom. But that wisdom was essentially a perfecting, a ripening, a mellowing process. There was none of the excitement and liberation an American student might feel at a university, with the right teacher or friends, for that would be a liberation from a small narrow world into a much larger one with many different levels, some of them stretching away above him. British students have been gradually removed from that old narrow world from the age of eleven. For them the university is merely the crystallization, the materialization of what had been only mental, the ideal community yearned after by their teachers. That is the extraordinary glamour of Oxford and Cambridge, their unreality, the way one knows, long before one gets there, that it will soon be over, and that one will always yearn back to it; three golden years when every unpleasant fact is excluded, and only the pleasant facts count, intelligence, manners, high spirits, charm, wit, beauty. A glamorous world, but static and rigid, the essential limits foreknown; the discoveries are all of the recondite, the recherché, the exquisite; the brilliant conversation is self-conscious sophistry. Of course, some of the students are serious, but not the most intelligent. Of course, some rebel against the dominant mood, but they are the deliberately eccentric, the Bohemian. For we had all learned at school how much and how little enthusiasm can accomplish, how long a new idea remains valid, how everything that is, and can be, under the sun, has lived there and died there before. At the university this takes almost material form; one is steeped, as it were, in a heavy concentration of wisdom, which eats away at any stubbornness or crudity of enthusiasm, any active dissatisfaction or sense of difference. It is an extremely articulate and perfectly self-confident wisdom—remember it has *all* the brightest people in the country within it. There is no one left outside to criticize. It exerts a very firm, an inescapable control.

At twenty-one, with my B.A. from Cambridge, I faced the world completely transformed, a gilded youth; knowing it was gilt, but the best gilt, and wasn't that better than bare tin? I stood in a small group, point O something or point OO something of my contemporaries, who practically monopolized all the best jobs in the British Council, the Foreign Service, UNECO, the BBC, the Colonial Service, the administrative grades of the Civil Service, teaching, the universities, publishing, the educated press, the Church, the Army, Navy, and Air Force, all the vantage points from which our manner and our mind could impress themselves on the country and the world as the educated way to be, as "Britain."

Certainly there are other systems which produce gentlemen. Those born into the right families and incomes, those who go to the public schools, become the real thing much less self-consciously. The provincial universities, unable to be anything different from Oxford and Cambridge, produce their own slightly more depressed, deprecatory, and charlatan gentlemen. The training for medicine and law, all the professions, gives the manner. Music and the theater demand it from their members; Sir Thomas Beecham, Sir Malcolm Sargent, Sir Laurence Olivier, Sir John Gielgud are thoroughly gentlemen. And indeed everyone in the country, from the crudest social climber to the most sensitive seeker of education and distinction, is bound to ape it sooner or later.

III

All of which wouldn't be half so tragic if the "British" mind weren't dead, no longer able to deal adequately with reality, its modes of apprehension a dead shell, an old skin to be sloughed. This became vivid to me the other day at *The Colditz Story*, the story of a German prison camp, written by one of the inmates, and made into a movie with actors of considerable ability and training, Eric Portman and John Mills, which yet presented the Germans as all gross like Goering, or ratlike as Goebbels, all violent and overbearing and humorless, and the British as all lighthearted and clean-limbed, boyish, larking about, ruffling their hair, baffling their captors by their irresponsible good humor. There is no echo of the reality of war—no hint of real hatred, real boredom, real terror, real cruelty—only schoolboy magazine equivalents. There is no reality in the relations between the English prisoners; not even the transmuted echo of that reality caught in *Stalag 17,* a more simply comic film. In even a second-rate American actor you feel the allusion to the unspoken parts of his personality—the gross, the sensual, the brutal. But in these sketches there is no allusion, it is all neatly excised, and you are left with something as dry and sweet as a whiff of lavender, as near a human being as a fashion sketch of 1910. The conventions of British characterization have scarcely advanced since then. In *Reach for the Skies,* after a heavily "psychological" approach to the hero's competitiveness, *from birth,* we are suddenly asked to accept his daring in war as an attempt to rise above the disability he acquired in manhood. I don't think you would get such radical confusion in an American film; not one made with as good an actor as Kenneth More. There have been a dozen American films, made without distinguished actors or directors, that have caught more of the violence, the disgust, and the monstrousness of war.

The British mind has not yet assimilated the First World War, never mind the Second. The line between officers and men makes both groups unreal to the imagination, forces them into false categories, the gentlemen and the sons of toil, with neither of whom one can wholly identify himself. I said before only the character with the BBC accent is taken seriously. I should have said "most seriously." In fact, any mode of speech in England is an accent, suggesting a type, with all its limits, weaknesses, sterilities. Marlon Brando or Montgomery Clift can play someone of the poorest class and education in such a way that you can forget those facts; you don't have to forget them, you are never really conscious of them. That's just what can't be done in England. That is why an artist can produce only a gross caricature of war; or, of course, an essentially private picture. He can't unself-consciously live the life of the people involved. Wilfred Owen's and Robert Graves's protests against the complete failure in England to understand what the First World War was are fully valid today, down to details. The heroic lies of 1914 were not told again in 1939, but we had only the deprecatory humor of *Mrs. Miniver* instead. Hemingway's and Dos Passos's protests in America were much more effective; James Jones and Norman Mailer had at least learned that lesson. The Second World War was presented to America as war. But in England the injunction against shouting was stronger than the need to capture and express vital experience.

Moreover the failure of a British film, one made with talent, like *The Colditz Story,* is much more serious than the failure of the equivalent in America is. Eric Portman, Kenneth More, John Mills talk and dress, and I'm sure think, much more like an M.P., an editor of the *Times,* a BBC announcer, etc., than John Wayne does his equivalents. It doesn't much matter if John Wayne is absurd. Nobody is supposed to take him seriously. He in no sense represents the educated mind of his country. Eric Portman does. At the end of the film, as the British commanding officer, he brings a courtyard of boisterous soldiers to order with two quiet words, reads them a message from escaped comrades, in cool defiance of the Germans standing by, and walks away from the camera over the cobblestones, hands in pockets, melancholy, distinguished, omniscient, and everyone in the courtyard, and the cinema, is obviously supposed to watch in quiet tense admiration and sympathy—thirty seconds' worth. And yet I'd swear no intelligent Englishman, of whatever education, could *honestly* feel that sympathy. It's too old a trick, too obvious, too self-satisfied. Too old a trick in life as well as in the film.

But we will not reject it in life. We know it's a trick but we don't believe there is anything else more genuine. The "British" mind works in self-conscious clichés, as a conversational technique, and, at the deepest level, in the large dramatic matters, love, war, duty. It must surely have puzzled Americans that young English people, graduates of universities, talk and act like characters out of Agatha Christie. Agatha Christie, after all, has always openly dealt in clichés, and uses the same ones now as at the beginning of her long career. But to us all the possible varieties of behavior are neatly categorized, all their weaknesses and absurdities equally well known; to choose any other than the "British" would be pointless, unless one is a "character." It's another part of the feeling at the university I mentioned, that all the important possibilities have been explored and measured; there is only the rather amusing, rather interesting, rather touching, left.

Of course the "British" mind has been active since 1910. But I suggest that its development has been dominated by a discovery of the religious approach to life. More exactly, the religious retreat from life. Much the dominant figure, after all, has been T. S. Eliot. The only other prophet of equal size, D. H. Lawrence, has been neglected precisely in measure as he stood in the opposite direction from Eliot. Eliot's success is the same thing as Lawrence's neglect. The political movement of the thirties was a failure, from every point of view. Our themes have been and are Sin, Doubt, Catholicism, Horror, the Limits of Human Goodness; our whipping boys, enthusiasts, liberals, optimists, noncomformists. We have learned to see the world as hell à la Greene, and hell à la Waugh. Nobody has shown us a person we can admire and love dealing with life in a way we can admire and love.

The English imagination has been dominated by a feeling of death, decay and hopelessness, and by an aspiration to style and elegance. These feelings have, of course, been fed by recent history, particularly in its impact on Britain's economic and international position. Their effects can be seen in a glance at the cultural map. There is, for instance, the remarkably anti-American, pro-French orientation of most cultured British people. Writers of the kind the British call brilliant, like Wyndham Lewis and Iris Murdoch, are always the extremest exponents of this; Lewis's novel *Self-Condemned* is pathological in its virulence against the New World and its yearning after the wit and clarity and irony of France. The most important vein of feeling is that which runs from Eliot to Graham Greene, Angus Wilson, Evelyn Waugh, and those like him; in Greene the feeling of death is strongest; in Waugh, Anthony Powell, Nancy Mitford, William Plomer, Sybille Bedford, etc., the love of elegance— the Sitwells have the same Palladian aspiration. A complementary line of intellectual agility allied with avowed clichés of the imagination runs from *The Confidential Clerk* to Charles Williams, C. S. Lewis, Dorothy Sayers, Agatha Christie. All these writers portray gentlemen, strip them to absurdity, finally swaddle them in pity; "they are poor things, but they are the best humanity can do, so . . ." There are, of course, other orientations in the British mind, some of them opposite in tendency. I claim only that the one hinted at here is dominant.

Only this can explain the enthusiasm over *The Outsider,* which was really a humiliating incident for an Englishman. The reviews unanimously and wholeheartedly, with real generosity, praised it; they welcomed an important new writer. Reading them abroad, long before I could get hold of the book, I thought something important had happened. Somebody without any of the required training and manner had broken into the closed circle. Three weeks after the book was reviewed in the Sunday *Times,* Wilson himself was writing for the paper. His rise was meteoric and quite unprecedented. But by the time I was a third of the way through the book I realized the true explanation. Wilson is brilliant, Bohemian, eccentric, the genius. He is the permitted exception; sleeping on Hampstead Heath is the perfect touch for him; he is almost like one of those brilliant young Frenchmen. The book itself is inaccurate in detail and fraudulent in method to the point of being very bad. The reason these things were not detected by the reviewers is that it said what they wanted to hear; it justified them; it accumulated the evidence of all the great spiritual giants, from Dostoevski to Sartre, to prove life today impossible, normal happiness out of the reach of, beneath the dignity of, the sensitive man. Such words, from a young man in a turtle-necked sweater who sleeps out at night in a public park, are exactly the mark of the one non-"British" mode the "British" will accept.

We don't even want to be shown someone we can admire and love dealing with life in a way we can admire and love.

IV

When I went back to England last summer, after a year in Turkey, where I had seen and heard only "Britain," at the Embassy and the British Council and in the papers and books and on the radio and the screen, I wandered round London and Cambridge and the great monuments, extremely depressed. I was in a country of pygmies, deliberately affected and malicious. And then suddenly, without forethought, when I was visiting Wigan, I became aware that that feeling no longer rang true. The faces and voices of the people, their clothes, the buildings in the street, the atmosphere, the landscape, none of it was "Britain." It was a totally different country and people. "Britain" after all was a very small minority, and sharply distinct from the majority in nearly everything. Wigan was one huge tuning fork; lay it to your ear, and all the melodies at present playing are false. If only our writers would do that. But the revelation was twofold; these streets and people had their own note, to which you could tune your whole instrument. There is a positive social atmosphere, a kindliness, a sincerity, a shrewdness, stimulating those same qualities in you, making it a good place to live. If this Northern nature, this mode of being, could be educated, without being made "British," the English mind might move forward again, move freely, begin again to see and feel things freshly and vigorously.

It's plain enough, I think, where Evelyn Waugh, Nancy Mitford, Angus Wilson get the note they tune themselves to, the key in which they play; the stately homes and the great public buildings. It makes an unpleasant, affected treble. It's obvious, too, that there are many working-class neighborhoods which give off their own note, quite different from that of Wigan. I make no case for "the people"; I am more interested in the intellectual aristocracy. If I attack them, it is not for being an aristocracy, but for being a bad one, feeding their vitality from meager, polluted streams. There is no reason to suppose working-class places in general better than others. The suburbs of London, and the new towns, and all Surrey and Hertfordshire, most of the South of England, has its own note, one that our writers have caught well—Eliot, Auden, Greene, Spender, Mac-Neice, etc. There, more than anywhere in the world, the mass media have had their so often prophesied, so often lamented effect; everyone lives in the arc-lamp glare of the *Daily Express* and the Light Program and the Ice Rink and the Palais de Danse. All organic life is killed, and discriminating people weave baskets or go to live in Majorca. In those clean, wide, quiet streets you can hear that note very clearly, the note of conscious smallness, sameness, separateness, "Leave me alone and I'll leave you alone."

The reasons why the North is different are no doubt complex, but one may point out that the people of the North live among the really dramatic ruins of England. The castles and abbeys are no more alive to the imagination than Hollywood imitations, but those Northern industrial towns are smoking, blackened ruins of the great thrust of energy that swung the world on its pivot, flung us into the momentum and direction we are trying to control today. These are ruins that are still alive, and yet are soaked in local and national memories; that is living tradition. The charm of the English countryside is irredeemably "olde worlde," the towns are too pretty and trivial, the history is hopelessly in the hands of Olivier, but Wigan, Preston, Salford keep their intensity and freshness of impact, which is by no means simply, or even dominantly, ugliness. To live and move among those buildings is to be sharply challenged every day, to be held to a highly charged battery and tested, to suffer a strongly cauterizing touch on your purposes and passions.

It is there, in the North and Midlands, that British people can still be serious and spontaneous. But all the cleverest children every year are sent to school to be made "British," like an offering of first-born. All the best blood is fatally thinned.

64

England *must* break its dead shell, slough its old skin, or its young men will grow more and more consciously absurd, their minds will grow as pretty and useless as Chinese feet, more and more they will have nothing but will power to hold them together and make them move forward; all power of desire and response will dry up; nothing will be left but self-destructive and destructive irony.

NOTE: The types I have described are, of course, only examples. There are two or three other types of "Britisher" and of grammar school teacher, which might just as well be chosen, and which would amount to much the same thing. There are also some who seem to amount to something different. For instance, in *The Colditz Story* John Mills played a puppyish young officer with none of the constricted and constricting elegance I have suggested as characteristically "British": and who yet, I must admit, is a very "British" type. The answer is that that character will be the Eric Portman character when he grows older, or would like to be. He is under the domination of that idea. His variation from it is merely personal and accidental, the result of personal limitations, not at all intentional or decisive. None, as a matter of fact, of my teachers were much like the one I described. But they had moments, gestures, that were his, and at those moments they were pleased with themselves; his idea was in the air—in books, on the radio—and they were not significantly, intentionally, different. In every culture there are characteristic types; there are variations within each type, and there are several types, so that from the wrong point of view they shade off into ordinariness; but with varying degrees of intensity these seven or eight bear a charge of significance for that culture; they are the people it is good or bad to be. These are queerly shaped logical counters, I know, but I think they are solid and valid.

"'B*ritain' and Britain"* *appeared in January,*
1958, and rereading it I realized that I had let in a lot of light,
more, in a sense, than I had intended, on the darkness and
confusion of feeling that had so paralyzed my mind in, say,
France, 1951-52. A great many ominous shapes had disappeared
or shrunk into something recognizable and maneuverable.
There was no reason why I should like this, want that, laugh
at something else; so I needn't feel guilty if I didn't; I needn't
feel that the whole shape and poise of my personality were
inherently wrong. And the exhilarating thing was, of course,
that these hobgoblins and threatening angelic forms were not
just private hallucinations but generally accepted, socially ac-
credited things. I could point them out, and make them vanish,
for other people too. And then came the awareness of clear,
unambiguous distances and depths, the sense of locked muscles
unlocking, the general central stirring and stretching and dis-
covery of limbs, as I began to like this and want that of my own
initiative. How can people talk about the intellect as if it were
a mechanical, emotionless thing concerned only with abstrac-
tions and externals?

I also realized, on rereading, that I must follow up this idea
of national types, and their relation to a culture as a whole:
these were the ideas that best connected and summed up my

66

general thinking. But I still did not think of those ideas as essentially related to my personal problems, my exile. The liberating effect of my last essay I still found accidental, and, even more clearly, final. The intellectual link between that chapter and the next one I wrote seemed to me to have nothing to do with the old problem of England-and-myself. I felt I could go further along the path I had begun, widen the light-entering hole, by generalizing out, away from that personal predicament. I didn't think of "Cultural Images," the next essay I produced, as next in any series. It was to have been, rather, a new start, an escape from the old obsession.

For the circumstances of my life and new intellectual sympathies were giving me a distaste for, spoiling the glamour of, obsessions and predicaments and personal problems. Some of my deepest tastes were changing. Life in America—both my own discovered satisfaction and stability there and the national atmosphere of satisfaction and stability—was making me aware of new truths and new beauties. Things I had before dismissed as complacency or complaisance I now saw as kinds of realism or good will. Especially now that I was teaching at one of the Eastern colleges, and getting attuned to the more brilliant and self-confident intellectual temper of that society, I could no longer believe in as simple, as sharp, a dissatisfaction with established social arrangements. I began to see the beauty of success as well as of failure. I began to see that urbanity in John Crowe Ransom, for example, was something much more attractive and impressive than I had thought urbanity could be. In England I had found it easy, and safe, to dismiss academic urbanity as a sure sign of moral, if not intellectual, sterility. And I recognized in these new acquaintances, personal and literary, several kinds of polish and elegance which quite clearly involved no sacrifice of decency or acuteness or force. So I was anxious that my next essay should escape the limits of the parochial and the personal and the angry. I would have liked to achieve some impersonality, some freedom of pure, self-balancing intelligence.

But in the writing, the subject matter itself, as I discovered its true contours, its essential inevitable form, forced me back to my own experience, and to just that area of it I had written about before. And in point of fact, of course, it is only in this essay that I finally justify myself as not, in the earlier pieces, merely rehashing old inert commonplaces. In "Thoughts About Two Homes" I had leaned uncomfortably heavily on the democracy idea; in " 'Britain' and Britain," on the contrast between North and South. I had assured myself at the time that I was using both sets of terms mythically, not literally, but I was not entirely convinced that I had not merely wanted to seem more subtle than the average cultural sight-seer. In this essay I at last put my finger on what I am talking about: what makes democracy and the North mythically true for me, what their relation to the literal, conceptual truth is.

CULTURAL IMAGES IN
ENGLAND AND AMERICA

It seems to me that, in the nexus of relationship between the individual and the culture in which he develops, there is one most important factor, the cultural image, which I have never seen defined or discussed to my satisfaction. In fact, the cultural image seems to me *the* most important single mode of connection between the two, and therefore of mutual creation, for by means of it the society creates an individual, and the individual creates his society—an image being a concrete and dramatic version of an achieved life, in which you recognize yourself as you could be, your powers developed in some sense fully and harmoniously, dealing with your problems and responsibilities on the whole triumphantly; for—this is the crucial point—you respond to, revel in, *love* this mode of being.

For example, Pierre Bezhukov or Kostya Levin in Tolstoy's great novels were such images for the Russia of his time. Young men growing up there then, however different their temperaments and convictions from Tolstoy's, must at least have had the possibilities of life celebrated in a way they could not deny or doubt or fail to respond to, however different the use they intended to put them to.

Looking back on my own period of greatest growth, I think I can now trace all kinds of surprisingly personal frustrations and failures to the fact that my society, England, provided me with no adequate images. None good enough, that is, to excite me, arouse me, set me moving inside, growing, reaching out. For if there is no adequate image, if one cannot excitedly want to be the kind of man on whom, for instance, T. S. Eliot or J. B. Priestley sheds the greatest glamour, one may not want to be anything at all; one's most valuable energies, that is, may remain quiescent; one may not want to *be* at all—not, that is, with the intensity one is capable of, and unused intensities easily become perverse.

Of course, one has other sources of energy. We all find such images in our parents; and most of us in our schoolteachers; and then the newspapers and the television surfeit us with the heroes of local and national politics, and sports, etc., for us to model ourselves on. Religion offers us images every Sunday. However, any intelligent person is likely to discover in, say, Pierre and Natasha, a richness which is new to him, and to feel a *wholeness* of admiration he never felt before. He is likely to be more deeply excited, at the roots of his being, where changes begin, when he reads a novel like *War and Peace*. So that ultimately the responsibility for this feeling remains, immensely, with "high" culture.

The sensation, when I found such an image, I can remember to this day, because it was so unassimilable. It came at nineteen, when I read *Sons and Lovers*. I recognized myself, and I knew at once that I had never done so before, in Paul Morel; and in the Morel family life, for in an image the whole system as well as its single great product is important, the plant as well as the flower. It was a novel sensation. Not that I hadn't dismally acknowledged a kinship to, say, Aldous Huxley's central characters. This was a different kind of recognition. As a matter of fact, I had no illusions of any resemblance between Paul's and my temperament, experience, problems, or powers; as personality types go, I thought him antithetical. Nor was I converted by the "ideas" of the book. I'd read my Eliot, and I knew Romanticism when I saw it. My new recognition was feeling—

70

and in a major key; that above all, in a major key—"There, that's what I would have felt in Paul's situation." His situation including his temperament, etc. Or, "There, that's what I half-thought yesterday. It's *true*." And excitedly, tumultuously, "Ah, now, if marriage—or family life—or friendship—were like that —if it can be like that . . ." And most often, "That's what I do, or so-and-so does, all the time. It's *natural* to do that. It's *right*." I think before it had seemed to me, as no doubt to many adolescents, that a pleasant truth always turned out to be a platitude, or applicable only to others, and really convincing things were always grim.

I felt that for the first time I was reading about people like myself, but whose lives were in a major key, and I reached out into my own routines and difficulties, anxious to achieve something of the same kind for myself. This kind of excitement acts on the sources of life deep in one exactly as the sun and the rain act on the seed in the soil. But more creatively. The image not only excites the soul to life, it offers it the form it may take. The seed of a dandelion must grow into a dandelion if it grows at all. But the soul of a young Englishman may grow into several different things, according, very importantly (among cultural influences, *most* importantly of all), to the image under whose domination he first stirs to life. When I found my image, for instance, I began to grow into something asocial, if not anti-social. I more or less turned my back on money and jobs and public responsibilities and achievements of all kinds, even, in some real though not powerful sense, on politics and economics and government.

I was twenty-five before I discovered, by accident, that there was a job I liked to do. I had done things before, without resentment and without boredom, because I expected nothing more; but then I discovered—and it was a shock—that there was an activity I would be paid for, a job society wanted done, which I wanted to do. Which gave me a sense of exertion and satisfaction, of anticipation and retrospection, of involvement and power and co-operation, a grip on the fabric of public and historical experience, places and people and events, so that the stream of outer happenings did not merely pass me but was interwoven with my inner concerns to make a whole human life. All this was new to me; I had not had even an anticipatory taste of it; because I had had no image of myself in a social role.

I use myself only as an example. When we left school at eighteen, of the twenty-five boys in my sixth form, no more than two or three knew what they wanted to be. And this was not because we saw ourselves as Paul Morel, remember. That came later, to the one or two it ever came to. We just did not see ourselves as anything. (This did not make us unhappy, of course; we were not conscious of it; we didn't know you *could* see yourself as something.) We had no impetus, no ambition, beyond the merely acquisitive and self-assertive. And the novels of the Angry Young Men surely corroborate this point, and illustrate it very graphically. John Braine's and Kingsley Amis's heroes have no forward thrust, except personal ambition, no guiding ideal, except a general, in some ways vague, sense of decency.

So we were given no enthusiasm for life as a creative enterprise for mature beings. We were left to squat or to rot inside our imprisoning egos. I think this was partly because we were British, and partly because we were Anglo-Saxons.

The Anglo-Saxons have inherited the earth, culturally speaking. But by some strange law they have had to lose their soul in the process; for surely the soul of a nation, culturally speaking, is its image of its typical product as noble, numinous, charismatic. And no one thinks of Anglo-Saxon types as passionate, or profound, or beautiful; it is the subject, unsuccessful races we see in these roles, and the Anglo-Saxons are official, efficient, blank. But images of the fiery Irishman and the ascetic Hindu and the happy Polynesian are no adequate substitute.

We listen to albums of Bessie Smith, and feel our human nature enlarged and intensified, our powers of acceptance warmed and dignified; but at the same time we know that it is for Negroes in a far more intimate sense than it is for us. The voice and the virtues are all deeply Negroid, and can give their exact pitch and key only to Negro natures. Imitation is not the essence of responding to an image; but identification is. If you feel at some level that you are excluded where other people are included, the image becomes exotic. It may remain valid aesthetically, but culturally it becomes unreal.

For our image of passion we watch Anna Magnani. No Anglo-Saxon actress can give us a comparable picture of total commitment, every inch and pulse and hair of the body at one with every twist of feeling. No Anglo-Saxon actress can get as close to it as other Italian stars. I suppose our equivalents are Judith Anderson and Bette Davis; who, quite apart from their different talents, are distanced from the viewer by conscious artwork; they are our image of somebody being dramatic. But then we cannot be passionate ourselves in any way resembling Anna Magnani's, because her whole mode of consciousness is so foreign to us. We are excited, of course, but not as I was excited by Paul Morel. We can recognize ourselves in her only very distantly and coolly.

Our most effective image of modern family life is perhaps that seen at its most vivid in Clifford Odets's plays; characters and relationships of great vitality, the mother above all massively dominant, together combining an almost animal intimacy with each other with equally strong, and centrifugal, idealism; expressed in a dialogue both laconic and literary, highly idiomatic and highly unidiomatic at the same time. This image seems to be essentially Jewish. When Odets disguises it by making his characters Italian, Polish, or Greek, the strengths of the play are exactly those qualities which are clearer and more authentic in Jewish settings. Bernard Malamud and Philip Roth use this openly Jewish image in their fiction. Paddy Chayefsky uses it, transmuted, in Italian and Czech settings. Perhaps it can be nearly as authentically Italian as Jewish. The point is that it cannot be authentically Anglo-Saxon. When a writer attempts to present this image in Anglo-Saxon terms, as Arthur Miller does in *Death of a Salesman,* the peculiar inversions and clumsinesses of the language are bewildering and exasperating; the relationships are vaguely false and foreign; until you realize that this is really also a Jewish family.

These are powerful images; comparatively unlimited—by class, education, etc.—in their appeal. All people of the same race can recognize themselves in them and glory in them. But they are irrelevant, ultimately, or very limited in their effectiveness, even for Negroes, Italians, and Jews. For they too live in the Western world, which is moving forward, or on, under the dominance of Anglo-Saxon modes of consciousness. Latin passion, etc., belongs to the spectacle of life, not to its serious business, even for Latins. A girl of keen intelligence, whatever her racial heritage, cannot want to become like Anna Magnani; because she could never naturally say and do those things, see and feel things that way. Normal intelligence and education nowadays prevent it.

What Anglo-Saxon figures are there with any comparable breadth of appeal? What images, not disqualified by normal intelligence and education, health and ambition, etc.? What do normal education and ambition direct one toward? Probably Princess Grace and Prince Philip. The long, blond, and swanlike, the expensive and anonymous, with the gift wrapping still round them. They are the essence of Anglo-Saxonism (whatever their parents and grandparents may have been); intelligent, handsome, fortunate, spirited, well behaved, always in good taste.

And this kind of glamour is, of course, mere simonizing compared with what we were talking about before. The least intense glance convinces one he will never recognize himself in them. There is no excitement and no formation.

All Anglo-Saxons, American as well as British, are badly off in this way. The figures with general appeal which the average child is likely to come up against are all inadequate in one way or another. The child of a Jewish or Italian home can find his and his people's possibilities magnificently celebrated—temporarily. But in the long run, if he pursues his salvation with any intensity, that is, he must find that path nonviable.

And as the mass media more and more usurp the functions of more local sources of images, even in part the home, the cultural poverty must become more disastrous.

But images do not come only in single figures. They may be fragmentary, embodied in different ways for different groups, each fragment limited in its appeal to a particular class, even limited to particular virtues in a character, so that the entire personality is not underwritten. The villain of a story may display some typically American virtue at the end, which does not redeem him in our eyes, but which does help build up an image of "the American." Anglo-Saxon images especially seem to come in this form. This is no doubt because the image of oneself (and we are the essential self of the Western world) is always so difficult to achieve, so disturbing, so complex. One can round out a picturesque conception of a Russian peasant or a Negro slave so much more easily than one of oneself. The self is always in formation, resists categorization, is essentially unpicturesque. One sees this and that aspect of it rather than the whole.

There were, then, fragmentary images available to my friends and to me as we were growing up. No society can exist without creating images, and though I think the fragment is from this point of view always inferior to the whole image, still there's no doubt that America does not suffer from the same kind of blight as Britain. I think that, as British, we were offered unattractive choices.

(I am conscious always of how many other factors are operative in these conditions besides the one I mention, notably the expanding, in America, or contracting, in Britain, temper of economic and political life in the two countries, the historical consciousness of each, the world situation of each. But these factors make themselves felt partly *in* the images; so they are to that extent taken account of; and their force *outside* the images, I would assert, is weaker than the images themselves.)

In the images we had when we were growing up, the good things were so qualified, negated, by the bad things, the total being was so mutilated, that we could not respond to them.

I don't mean our *pictures* of, for instance, the suburban middle class as neat, cramped, respectable, harried; or of independent farmers as large, slow, hearty, rather primitive. These are *pictures,* not images, because they focus on limitations, or at best characteristics, not achievements and powers. There are pictures in every culture, with or without adequate images. I mean here our true images, those that had some real glamour, that could seem, unless one's life depended on it, versions of an achieved life. As an example I'd like to take the images of "authority" and "innocence," which are crucial and polar possibilities in America as well as in Britain, and perhaps in all Western culture. (Other examples of such polar pairs are "Protestant" and "Catholic," "instinct" and "reason," and "religious" and "humanist"; none of which seem to me as crucial as these two.) In both countries, at all levels of intelligence and seriousness, we find fragmentary images of the man of authority and the man of innocence; not in explicit opposition, for both are "good" figures, but presenting to us very different qualities as the most important ones. These are the forms which lie available to our ambitions and our moral sense as we decide, unconsciously, how firm and decisive it is good to be, how receptive and responsive, how efficient and how sensitive. It is our cultural images that make these alternatives crucial and concrete to us, limit them for us, give them meaning. A comparison of these polarities in American as well as British culture will help explain Britain's lack of vitality.

The two possibilities for Britain were picturesquely summed up in Olivier's movie, *Richard III,* where John Gielgud, as poor simple Clarence, was made such a fool of by Olivier. Gielgud is a superb figure of the British kind of innocence and spontaneity and sensitiveness; innocent, elegant, lyrical, unable or unwilling to defend or assert himself. He has had this quality in so many of the parts he does superlatively well that, as a cultural image, he *is* the quality. Even in middle age he keeps that flower-like freshness, uncallused and undergraduate; but with the pathos of a victim in it. While Olivier dominated the screen and the audience and life—by what? By sheer will power, by the negation of spontaneity. His Richard has no feeling, no thoughts, but self-assertion. He conquers by sheer force of will, fascinating the Lady Anne, confusing and hypnotizing his foes by such a concentration of purpose their own ruddier, comelier features fall apart, agape, made stupid. It is not that his hypocrisy deceives people, it is that they cannot account for him at all. He is not human. There is no compromise in him, no multiplicity of appetite, no need for human relatedness. When he pretends to be in love, she is not deceived, she is dazzled. By that brilliance in him which is joy in the defeat of humanity in others and in himself.

And in rendering this part Olivier brought out a quality which, we then realized, lies deep in most modern British figures of authority and intelligence that have any vividness, any impact—a quality of a revenge taken on one's own spontaneity. That quality has always been there in Olivier himself, for example; it is what made his playing of Hamlet and Henry V less than satisfactory; there is a vicious clarity, outline, and power in everything he does, like the crack of a whip. The same quality is there, surely, in Basil Seal, the only satisfactory Waugh hero, who brazenly, brilliantly, steals and lies and cheats his way through the most sacred human relationships, with his mother, his sister, the woman he loves. Basil is a blackguard but we enjoy him; we sympathize, while we read, even in his attack on human nature; because he is such a vivid figure, though fragmentary, of cleverness and self-reliance. The same quality is there, much sweetened, in Shaw's heroines: Candida, Lady Cecily, Ann Whitfield, Mrs. Higgins. In Professor Higgins and Caesar just as much. These again are brilliant figures of authority, and their brilliance is essentially a matter of managing other people's emotional lives. They themselves do not get too involved; they provoke other people into emotion and then— making them feel rather fools—neatly circumnavigate them, kindly, cleverly, humorously, making them do what is good for them. Low down the scale of complexity and intensity we find the same quality in Lord Peter Wimsey, who lightly and humorously convinces his sister she couldn't possibly be in love with a Socialist and whose own emotional life is all classical allusions and off-stage neurosis. High up that scale, there is Sir Henry Harcourt-Reilly, entirely unrelated to other people, in whose presence other people's emotional problems seem foolish, unimportant, tarnished. All these figures, I would claim, add up to a characterization of the British image of authority and brilliance. And the prime emotional source of the energy of these figures and the mental worlds in which they live is what? Certainly not any passionate interchange, any mutual fulfillment, with an equal; that is conspicuously lacking in them; the source of their energy is a cold joy in the defeat of humanity in themselves and in others. In varying measure, sometimes not very importantly, the same is true of the heroes of Nancy Mitford, Ivy Compton-Burnett, Angela Thirkell, Agatha Christie. I think the same quality can be felt pervasively and strongly in the work of Noel Coward, Graham Greene, Angus Wilson, Henry Green.

The sensitive young man you meet in the novels of Rosamund Lehmann, and Virginia Woolf, and Elizabeth Bowen, long slim graceful creatures, like deer, but abrupt, nervous, complicated. As an example in real life, take Middleton Murry, made up so entirely of sensibility and sincerity; take Stephen Spender, as he presents himself in *World Within World,* so feminine in his relations with Auden and Eliot, and all the men of force he came up against; take John Lehmann or the sensitive boys in the fiction of L. P. Hartley and Denton Welch, and so many autobiographies. For the physical type take Leslie Howard, Ivor Novello, so many of the open-necked young men on the backs of Penguins in the twenties and thirties. In some essential way all of them were unequipped to live in the world, and were from the beginning broken blossoms, blossoms in the dust. They had some real beauty, but the sort that at its bravest drew attention to its own fragility.

One does not, of course, have to be all one or all the other.

Most people, even some of those named, have a bit of the blossom and a bit of the thorn in them. They are compounds. But when you combine the two you are still dealing with the same materials. You are sensitive *and* brutal. In better times and places men don't have to be either.

I can think of a few figures, both of authority and innocence, which escape these caricatural distortions. Paul Morel, for instance, is a figure of innocence with no connotations of porcelain. But Lawrence was a rebel, a real rebel, who remains outside British culture; not a mock rebel like Shaw, who was accepted on his own terms—which were also theirs—by intelligent people. Lawrence will be accepted the day he is so far in the past that his power as an image fades, the day there is no challenge left *in* "on his own terms."

Since my day, of course, the Angry Young Men have appeared. But I think they represent no essential break with the past, in this matter. Their heroes are split by this same dichotomy, alternately sensitive and brutal, and their solutions are at best personal and precarious. Jim Dixon, for example, in *Lucky Jim,* in his relations with Margaret Peel before the story opens, seems to have been involved against his will, unable to resist, exposed by a morbid sensitiveness, pity, and honor; and in order not to be destroyed he reacts at times dishonorably and brutally (with Evan Johns, for example). And the figures of authority all these novelists introduce, Julius Gore-Urquart (in *Lucky Jim*), Vernon Gruffydd Williams (in *That Uncertain Feeling*), Sam Brown (in *Room at the Top*), all strike the reader as sinisterly cold and hard; as colder and harder than is acceptable in view of the writer's boyish enthusiasm for them. The old distortions of authority and innocence are at work.

When life presents itself in such shapes, the young bird does not peck at the shell. It huddles quietly to itself.

In America the figure of innocence has been a good deal discussed. Leslie Fiedler, for instance, has written a whole book about it (*An End to Innocence*) in which he claims that Americans are obsessed with innocence. But I think they are just as much obsessed with maturity, with masterfulness, readiness to take responsibility, and readiness even to seem cruel and indifferent in the cause of responsibility. How many movies we've had with the lonely man on the bridge winning all the sympathy, even—in good movies—against real challenges from the Cheery Good Nature he affronted, the Ordinary Guys who hated him, the Happy Innocent Kids he frightened, and other powerful ideals. The best-known example, perhaps, is the novel, *The Caine Mutiny;* there the fascination with authority and responsibility visibly arrests the novelist in mid-career, and makes him invert the whole structure he had labored at till then. Tom Keefer, the intellectual, who had been extremely sympathetic till then, suddenly became the villain; and Captain Queeg, without ceasing to be odious, became a sort of hero. Why? Because he had been responsible, had taken authority all those prewar years the other characters, and the writer, and the readers, had been at best innocent.

This case was exceptional, because war experience obviously had upset the writer's earlier, more natural, scheme of values. But this type of situation is just what Hollywood has long excelled in handling. Stars, directors, script writers have all been at their best in problems of discipline, and courage, and command. Gary Cooper, John Wayne, Humphrey Bogart, Henry Fonda, Gregory Peck, Edward G. Robinson are not all brilliant actors, but they have all given us some fine passages on this theme—authority, necessary brutality, deliberate rejection of sympathy. It is these qualities that characterize the figure of authority in America. He appears in Westerns, gangster and historical, as well as war, films; always the hero is taking control, knocking people down to maintain authority, outraging the heroine and the young men with an insolence they learn to understand and love.

The same figure is easily recognizable at much higher levels of culture. Hemingway's situations and heroes center round this idea of authority. The toughness, the will to control, the loneliness, the power to take dislike, the distrust of all idealism, enthusiasm, optimism, and gush, all this specifies the "talent" of Colonel Cantwell, Wilson the hunter, Jack Brennan the boxer, Harry Morgan the gun runner. They seem amoral, but they all take the burden of control on their shoulders, the responsibility for others. Faulkner's moral world has the same orientation. It is dignity and authority the author celebrates, in Dilsey, in the Marshal, in Mr. Compson, in old Colonel Sartoris. Young men in Faulkner are crude creatures, compounded of animalism and idealism, needing to be tempered by age and experience. The brilliant image he presents is the one of authority. And in James Gould Cozzens, again, the glamour is all for the old, the wise, the established: Colonel Ross and General Nichols in *Guard of Honor,* Julius Penrose and Arthur Winner Senior in *By Love Possessed;* those who have seen through every emotion and expectation to pure reason, and pure solitude in arranging others' lives.

All these fragmentary figures add up, I would claim, to a very impressive image of authority, which can excite and form the powers for life of young Americans; far more, at least, than the other image of authority I discussed. It has more manliness than the British version, is less vengeful an attack on natural happiness and fulfillment, has less conceit and cleverness and more chance of some valid human relatedness. There is more natural healthy humanity in, say, John Wayne in *The Searchers* than in Eric Portman in *The Colditz Story.* There is a far more positive value in Wilson in "The Short Happy Life of Francis Macomber" than in the Englishman of Graham Greene's *The Quiet American.*

The image of innocence in America is a very brilliant one; it takes disparate forms, in *From Here to Eternity,* J. D. Salinger, Marlon Brando, "Billy Budd," Mark Twain, James Dean, Fitzgerald, and Henry James; but all, in their different ways, are mourning over the moment of adjustment to the adult world of compromise and insincerity. Huck Finn's innocence has a character of ignorance set beside Holden Caulfield's, but it is sophistication that is the great evil for both of them, and it is the purest innocence they both cling to in the figures of Jim the slave, Holden's sister Phoebe, and the nuns. It is the problem of corruption and their relation to it that tortured James Dean and Marlon Brando, in some of their best scenes, just as much as Isabel Archer and other of James's heroines. It is the moment cynicism becomes comfortable and unconscious they are all weeping over, fighting off, protesting against. This image of innocence is characterized by a great splendor of vitality, and intelligence, and positive achievement.

By contrast, the British image seems all the more frail, requiring protection on every side in order not to suffer. They can live only among each other, the most sensitive and beautiful, and even then life is too rough for them. Middleton Murry's life with Katherine Mansfield is a tragicomic example. It is not that such people are weak; they are genuinely fine-drawn, but to the point of uselessness. This kind of thing is perhaps nearer to Blanche Dubois in *A Streetcar Named Desire* than to Huck Finn. American innocence differs above all because it can include toughness—without ceasing to be innocence. Its figures suffer from the corruption of the world, but they can handle its crudities. You need only set Holden Caulfield beside L. P. Hartley's Eustace or Brando beside Gielgud, to be convinced. The Americans' relation with the world is much less predominantly aesthetic.

In short, the American images, of both innocence and authority, are whole men, whole lives, and the waking mind responds to them with some thrust of enthusiasm. The British images—and perhaps the same is true of most European cultures—are mutilated. Response to them must be feebler, and imitation a disaster.

This is no doubt the effect, but I think it is also the cause, of a generally inferior vitality.

America is better off than Britain; and is in a generally healthy condition culturally, from this one, and very important, point of view. Nevertheless she is impoverished, in having only

82

fragmentary images. Fragmented images are like diffracted light, diffuse, comparatively ineffective. Huck Finn, for example, embodies his innocence in a form almost as irrelevant to our immediate needs as Anna Magnani's passion. A boy cannot long grow upward into Huck Finn—or into Marlon Brando. Faulkner's Dilsey and the Marshal are self-conscious aesthetic devices; while you are reading their speeches and actions you are aware that it is the author who is telling you something by means of them; they themselves do not fill the eye and absorb the attention, and I could not respond to them as I did to Paul Morel.

The truly rich culture offers its members some choice of images that are whole in themselves, magnificently real, and keenly relevant to the time and place and situation of the young reader. The supreme examples of such images and of an image-maker are the two great novels of Tolstoy and Tolstoy himself. The heroes, Bezukhov and Levin, and the families they marry into, the Rostovs and the Shtcherbatskies, embody a way of life that is not so much depicted as celebrated. Other characters are depicted, as in Flaubert and George Eliot; figures like Vronsky and Bolkonsky, whom the author admires, and marvelously "understands," but who don't have the special Tolstoyan glamour; even Anna herself remains half within an aesthetic dimension Besukhov escapes. And the central characters and their family lives are presented as not merely good but "natural," "Russian." There are sharp *pictures* of the Frenchman, and the German, and the Englishman. And somehow we are made to feel that Alexey Karenin, or Alexey Vronsky, or Sergey Koznishev are less "Russian" than Levin—the "Russian" man being big, enthusiastic, simple, clumsy, stammering, manly, fatherly, loving, unpractical, moody, religious, intuitive.

The families are conscious of themselves as images. Denisov in *War and Peace* and Levin in *Anna Karenina* fell in love with the entire set of Rostovs and Shtcherbatskies. They loved the individual members indiscriminately, and with the same emotion; because it was the family life itself that attracted them, the mode of relationship, its tone of spontaneous gaiety, of natural goodness, of vitality and fertility. And the individual members feel the same way. The Rostovs all look silently at Vera every time she speaks—because she spoils their tone. Tolstoy asks us to fall in love with them in a precisely comparable way. And we do, if we respond to the novel at all properly. We want to marry and have a family like that, with the same *degree* of vitality, and, unless we see ourselves as radically different, with the same *kind* of vitality. And just as much he asks us to love his heroes. We feel we have only to open our hearts as Levin's or Bezukhov's is open, and follow its dictates as passionately, as ready as they to fall into absurdity, and we will achieve the same full-blooded, wholehearted innocence, the same salvation. Of course, when we put down the book here and now, we find none of the institutions, the modes of relationship, the modes of being we could deal with in this new role. It remains a great novel, but as an image it fades, becomes distant, romantic.

This was image-making on the grandest scale, and young men growing up in Russia in the same era had perhaps greater opportunities than any comparable group. They were roused and persuaded into life more irresistibly, more richly and melodiously, more deeply and thunderously, than any others I can think of.

And it is interesting for an Englishman to reflect that Russia at that time was in no flourishing condition politically, economically, or internationally.

No doubt it was easier for the Russians than for us. They were far enough from, and near enough to, the van of human progress, so that they could see the ways in which they differed, their "picturesqueness," without feeling it an inferiority. But is it impossible we should have the same?

It is clear enough what a phoenix a writer of similar temperament would be, who could create a whole image for Anglo-Saxons, in which people of the greatest intelligence and sensitivity could recognize themselves, and find themselves therein transformed, valuable and beautiful.

I want to suggest that America has such a phoenix in J. D. Salinger.

This is not the place to demonstrate Salinger's purely literary merits. I can only assert that he passes every test the reader's mind imposes, and enters it deeply enough to act upon the faculties of self-creation. The more you read him, the more original you find his meanings; the more he points out to you what you had not seen in your daily life, the finer and more vital his taste and tact are, the more exciting his intelligence and his complex tension of values. With each reading one salutes more perceptions and organization of perceptions, more penetration; and these salutes act as surrenders of the sensitive mind, the end of resistances and measurings, an opening of those secret areas where one's undirected eagerness and responsiveness lie undefended and indefensible.

But measured by such standards alone Salinger is not a phoenix. We have had as fine writers in our time, and one or two greater. He is no prophet, no D. H. Lawrence. When he approaches that function, in the expositions of Seymour's brand of religion, he becomes less distinguished. He has done nothing to equal the Leopold Bloom part of *Ulysses*. But he is an unparalleled image-maker; because he works essentially through central characters, who live in their own right, independently of the story, and who are beautiful and lovable; Holden Caulfield, Buddy Glass, Zooey Glass. After reading *The Catcher in the Rye*, for instance, one can ask oneself what Holden would say of this and that, what he would do in such a situation, and one can get an answer. Heaven knows how! This is the special miracle of the image-maker. And one rejoices in everything he would say and do, however painful for him, because of the integrity and the sweetness and the vigor of the nature that acts.

When Salinger does not write through such a central character, and the pattern of the writer's sensibility is imprinted on the narrative and action as it were nakedly, his work is much inferior. *Nine Stories,* for example, and even "Franny," seem to me relatively uninteresting. There is a bitterness like a wound in Salinger's mind, an expectation of disaster for anyone sensitive and innocent, which invalidates so much of a story like "Teddy" and "A Perfect Day for Bananafish." But in *The Catcher in the Rye* Holden's own qualities and life-worthiness remain in our mind, contradicting the pattern of failure and meanness; he, after all, cannot be seen through; he is not phony, nor, importantly, defeated. It is this that gives the book much of its poise and integrity.

All the way through *The Catcher in the Rye*, the reader, if he is honest and generous, is becoming aware of Holden's superiority. Each episode, each word in the book, has many "points," but this is the point of each of them, as much as anything else. Holden is taller, handsomer, more lovable, more loving, more intelligent, more honest—than whom? Than the reader. Than the writer, one can say; it is he who projects this image for us, from this angle, the effect of which is to make us wholeheartedly admire and love his character. At the very beginning, Holden is looking at his school, "trying to feel some kind of a good-by. I mean I've left schools and places I didn't even know I was leaving them. I hate that. I don't care if it's a sad good-by or a bad good-by, but when I leave a place I like to *know* I'm leaving it. If you don't, you feel even worse." The reader must feel that such glimmerings as he had at sixteen of the value of experience as such were never so exactly defined, so unpretentiously phrased, so socially amenable, so completely assimilated into his private language. Next comes the interview with the Spencers, where Holden is so easily aware of all they are thinking and feeling, while they are quite unaware of him, and he so charitably makes the interview easy for them. Again the reader must feel that such social dexterity as he had at sixteen was never so unself-conscious, so unpatronizing, so allied with humor and gaiety and kindness. And so on through the book; Holden's skill at golf, at dancing, at writing, his generosity with money, his enterprise with women, his ability to talk to children—one of the major dimensions by which all

86

these are measured is his superiority in them. The point of them all is that we look up to Holden.

Zooey Glass is even more flamboyantly endowed. A brilliant actor, a very forceful personality, a Greek scholar, a mathematics scholar, unusually beautiful, unusually serious, unusually sardonic and irreverent and impatient; on every side he exceeds and awes us. We feel that were we to meet him, or Holden, we would be overborne. At the same time, we long to meet them. We long to be a part of that complex of interchanges that makes up the Glasses' family life and the Caulfield children's relationship: each member wildly free and independent, and yet deeply devoted to the others: we want to inhabit that world whose every object is so richly significant, every movement or inertia so full of energy. The brilliance of the writing is to be measured by the way it makes acceptable to us something we cannot in the least patronize, makes us love someone before whom we cannot but feel timidity and insecurity about ourselves. This is what the writer is most deliberately making us feel. When he fails, with Seymour, it is precisely because we rebel against the demand for so much reverence, so wholly upward a glance. But when he succeeds, his characters have a natural, unqualified glamour which puts him with Tolstoy, not with Lawrence or Joyce. After *Sons and Lovers,* Lawrence no longer worked importantly in "character," no longer allowed his readers a big emotional relationship with the central figures. Bloom, on the other hand, though a big character, is not one we look upward to; the glamour in *Ulysses* is monopolized by Stephen Dedalus, who is unacceptable on so many other grounds, but who "could have been" much more comparable to Zooey.

So Salinger is definitely an image-maker, a celebrator, not a depicter. But it may seem that the life he celebrates is un-"achieved"; that Zooey and Holden have more problems than solutions, more weaknesses than strengths. This is true only from a point of view unsympathetic to the author; and from such a point of view the same is true of Levin and Bezukhov. Such an attitude can be justified; but only by literary criticism, by proving that Salinger and Tolstoy are not to be taken seriously as writers. From Salinger's point of view, his characters are strongly and vividly alive. So that as long as we acknowledge the value of his insights, his sensibility, they are strong and triumphant for us too. It is true *ob*jectively that his talent is narrow and tortured beside Tolstoy's; the setting, the action, the characters, the problems, the moods—the American writer's total output is only like some of the scenes involving one of the aspects of Bezukhov, who is as a totality only a part of *War and Peace.* Again, however, the objective view is irrelevant. It is the image-maker's privilege that we come to see with his eyes, from inside his work. After all, T. S. Eliot's work has not been notable for breadth or typicality, but it has had a powerful effect.

In Salinger's characters, Wellesley and Harvard undergraduates can recognize themselves transfigured, more intensely alive, more honest, more passionate, more courageous; they are caught up into a mode of being that exhilarates them by its pace and gusto; they reach out into their own routines and difficulties, anxious to achieve something of the same kind for themselves. In other words, they respond to a cultural image. One of the greatest of cultural miracles is taking place.

I said that Salinger was an image-maker for Anglo-Saxons. It remains to be seen how accessible his work is to Englishmen. Perhaps they will feel themselves as excluded from participation, as unable to identify, as with Clifford Odets's characters. Certainly Salinger is so much of his time and place, New York and that decade, that there will have to be an act of translation; and certainly the man who can redefine this kind of meaning in English terms will need a talent almost comparable to Salinger's own. Nevertheless this seems to me the best chance for English literature, English culture, today.

B y now, I sometimes felt, I bestrode the prostrate dragon easily, lashed and lanced it with impersonal precision; "Britain," as a personal problem, was mastered, and could do my first twenty-four hours there were proofs enough of the per- a dead horse. But when I went home for the summer of 1958 my first twenty-four hours there were proof enough of the per- sisting, powerful nature of the problem: no formula, no theo- retical understanding, would ever annul it.

An English publisher had written to me after " 'Britain' and Britain," saying that if I wrote a book along the same lines he would like to see it. My first reaction was that I should not let my- self be distracted from my true interests, which were represented by "Cultural Images"; it still did not occur to me that all these pieces belonged together, that the curve connecting all four was the curve of my true interests. However, as I prepared to go home, the thought came to me—it seemed to me rather cun- ning, rather tough-minded—that I might try to see if he would accept these pieces I had already written as parts of this book. So I roughed out a plan of what other topics I would expect to deal with in such a book; notably those things, those people, in English life which did seem to me to be still life-giving; and made an appointment with him for the day I arrived in England.

My plane got into London early in the morning, and I had

had no sleep. The sky is dark for only about four hours on that flight at that time of the year, and my brain was too excited by the thought of going home to take advantage of them.

Then everything along the bus route into the city upset me. The houses seemed so small, and the flower-bordered front paths, down which men in three-piece suits came hurrying off to work, seemed too bright and neat and prepared. Men were carrying umbrellas, whistling errand boys on bicycles were weaving in and out of the traffic, bright orange tile roofs curved gaily over pebbled-ash fronts. Bay windows, broad clean pavements, narrow, tarmacked roadways, lurching buses, everything was just as it was in the Ealing comedy movies. It was all nice and wholesome and harmless.

Sulphuric little messages, from the organs of guilt and shame, hurried along my blood stream to my stomach, my eyes, my heart, my brain. Nothing in England looked real to me. I could only think that everything was very cute; it was the ultimate blasphemy. I had then completely ceased to be English, completely severed my connections with all that I had been, all I most naturally was. That was myself out on the street I was looking at; hurrying along with his glasses sticking out of his breast pocket; that perfect piece of wavy-haired, hollow-chested, seedy gentility—I couldn't see the man less picturesquely, try as I would—that crumpled, pin-striped frontispiece to a Graham Greene novel. And if that was myself, what had happened to the thinking, feeling me? For I could no more imagine what it was like to be him than to be an Eskimo.

The publisher backed out of the position he was nervous he might have adopted, of encouraging me to write a book. What he had wanted, it turned out, was an Angry-Young-Man kind of diagnosis and denunciation; he found "Cultural Images" and the new ideas I outlined for him overambitious. If I went ahead and wrote the book anyway, I should bring it to him to see, but he felt bound to tell me that D. H. Lawrence and F. R. Leavis were two writers he found boring and profitless. However, he seriously assured me, publishers do sometimes rise above their private prejudices in their public function. This did not upset me so much, though it was depressing to see that what I had taken to be no man's land was, in fact, occupied by the enemy. But in explaining his change of attitude, he kept pointing out that as just another expatriate critic, my name had no particular prestige in England, to carry the book; there were dozens of expatriate writers, he reminded me, sniping at England from a safe distance. I certainly was expatriate; the word doesn't seem, now, so very loaded a term; but that morning, in my weakened condition, it struck home, heavily, and tore a large jagged hole in my conscience. I started listing heavily to port. Perhaps this whole structure of ideas about England and America was mere self-justification, this whole life in America a coward's retreat, dishonorable self-protection. A few making-conversation remarks, as he tied up a neat bundle of my manuscript for me to take away, like "Do they let you dress like that when you teach, over there?" and I abandoned ship completely. I admitted everything; I was an underbred, hangdog, name-calling, Americanized deserter of a sinking ship. A pleasant-faced, diffident young man, he was, with a part-hesitant, part-absent-minded manner.

In an hour or two I was piloting a rented car through the streets of London and north, toward home. The cars, the fields, the villages, the roads, everything I saw was so charming, so complete, I wanted to add it to a collection, somewhere. Where I ate my ham-sandwich lunch, two commercial travelers in crumpled suits were arguing old-manishly in the shiny, echoing lounge, while a mustached man in bold tweeds with a matching cap leaned sideways on the bar and drank from a tankard reflectively.

By the time I got to Tewkesbury, though it was only four

in the afternoon, I began to realize that I should not drive any further. Though I felt calm and clear enough in the conscious part of my mind, that seemed a narrower, frailer area than usual, and its floor was perceptibly heaving and howling. So I parked my immaculate, hired Austin (the brightest thing in Tewkesbury, with a "Visitor to Britain" sticker on the windshield) outside an old hotel, and took a room at the end of a dark, multileveled, spasmodic corridor, slippery with a hundred years of Mansion Polish, and ambushed at every corner with a spinning wheel, a warming pan, or a candlestick snuffer. Every detail of the furniture of my room, and of the servants' manner, announced that this was an old-fashioned place, where the old ways were still preserved, a corner of the old England saved from the hurry and harshness of modern life. I decided not to unpack, since I was so tired I could scarcely keep my eyes open, though at the same time my hands were trembling with excitement. The sense of guilt and agitation, restimulated by everything I'd seen and heard that day, had poisoned all my blood by now. Here was England, charmingly picturesque, perfectly sure of herself and satisfied with herself; absolutely excluding me, baffling even my imagination; I could not even understand any longer what it was like to live here and be English; I had just been barking round her heels like a pariah dog. All my mental and nervous machinery seemed speeded up to more than normal pitch, while my physical and facial muscles were slowed down, as if drugged. I felt as if I were developing a case of spontaneous combustion. However, I took a drink of the brandy I had bought at Shannon and went to bed.

I woke unusually alert and lively, and was surprised to see it was broad daylight; I must have slept fifteen hours. I went to the window to make sure at least my car, my thirty-pieces-of-silver worth, hadn't been stolen. I looked at my watch, puzzled, started to dress, went back to the window, thought a while, and gradu-

ally convinced myself. It was twenty-five minutes since I had fallen asleep.

I took another drink of brandy, and walked up and down the room for half an hour, and lay down again. I was by now terribly tired, but the wheels of my brain were spinning round faster than ever. So I took another, longer drink, and breathed deeply and slowly, and gradually, gradually, sleep came over me. An hour later I was awake again, bursting with energy, practically in orbit, ready to zoom moonward at a moment's notice. And that happened three more times, while Tewkesbury gradually got darker and quieter and emptier and put out its lights, until the only living thing in the street was me peering palely out of my window.

In the morning I was normal. The white corpuscles had won out. And though everything in the street still looked doll-like, I could convince myself it wasn't my fault. France and Turkey looked small and shabby after America, but not so consciously so. Britain played the part. She said she was "olde worlde," and cute, and not life-size. It was she who compared herself to America, not me; she who relegated herself to the status of artwork; my treachery, my Americanization, was being unable to believe, at first sight, in such a voluntary self-dramatization and self-diminishment.

It was even, in the long run, encouraging to see how formidable and how direct the antagonism was, between my sense of life and Britain's present idea of herself: how the texture of my most casual experience there renewed my sense of something wrong, and most untheoretically, most organically; so that the elaborate structure of thought I had been building up was not only corroborated but most powerfully confirmed in its necessity.

What was most necessary now was to seek out those elements of English experience which were solid and satisfying and char-

acteristic, in however different ways; those elements which gave me the sense of something wrong with the rest; and to work out the relationship between those different things. I had to get past the idea of democracy and the Northerner and the working-class man, to some more achieved and powerful cultural image in which I could see England as a whole. I had to find a voice, a manner, a career, a way of living, that would seem characteristically English to me, and genuinely exciting.

BRITISH DECENCY

1. F. R. Leavis, 1958

The sky was inky gray, the gravel paths gleamed wet and brown, and the buildings were a smooth wet featureless buff color round the broad blank lawns; in the emptiness the noise from the street sounded lost and small. Hearing something I turned, and Dr. Leavis had ridden up behind me, and was swinging down from his bicycle—which looked as big and shabby as ever—and which he then picked up under his arm, not looking at me, and hurried up the steps into the hallway, carrying it. I introduced myself. He was panting slightly, his hair and clothes were rough, disheveled, his mannerisms were all abrupt and flurried, but his manner, you gradually realized, was perfectly assured; and still flexible, answering to every element, every possibility, in what was, after all, a difficult social situation.

In my last glimpse of him, ten years ago, as a departing undergraduate, he had been on a bicycle. Lying in the long grass on the Backs, wondering what the experience of Cambridge had been, I glimpsed him, and pulled myself up, involuntarily; he and his wife and three children on bicycles of varying sizes, in irregular squadron, like a flock of starlings, proceeding along Queen's Road with their attentions concentrated on the lights, not solemnly or self-consciously, but with an intensity and seriousness and shabbiness which would have made them discordant with Cambridge in May, if it hadn't made Cambridge discordant with them. For the experience had been nothing but him, a pointless fancy-dress party, a velvet-glove shop for a world of unredeemed and ugly fact, a nothing but for him.

95

I listened to him even more than to what he said, back now in 1958. It was his voice even more than his words, the odd nasal accent and tones and rhythms, the peculiar range; which yet manages to include, to account for, everything. Monotonous, almost exhausted, and relentless, with tenor upper notes, and tricks of dying out, falling away, vocal shruggings; all given a nasal resonance almost like an organ in a church. And the amazingly brown and weather-beaten and vigorous face of someone who doesn't belong indoors; so deeply tanned—by the wind, not the sun—it would stay the same now if he were kept in bed ten years. His eyes, under tufted eyebrows, have the glare of someone who has seen the truth, and keeps his gaze fixed on it, but also the used, chiseled, hammered look of infinite adjustments and double checking, often fierce and nerve-racked. The careless, longish hair has receded now from the domed forehead, but the shabby shirt was still open low down on the chest; and as a whole, though marked with age, the fine-drawn, smallish features and limbs and body, as he lay slightly sprawling in his chair, his head back, talking, abounded in sanity and vigor and masculinity and Britishness. That was what I mostly heard.

He was intensely and integrally British. Not Europeanized, not of the intelligentsia, not of the upper classes, not of Bohemia, not of Bloomsbury, not of any group or set. Intensely private, as father and husband and critic and thinker, flesh and spirit bearing the marks of the same strenuous self-discipline, the same rejection of all "official" influence, he comes to us from generations of decency and conscience and reasonableness and separateness, of private houses hidden behind hedges, along the road from Matthew Arnold and John Stuart Mill, the road which took its most recent, still abortive, turning under the direction of D. H. Lawrence. Alone in all Cambridge his voice has echoes of the best things in my parents' England, makes connections between all the parts of my experience.

I went merely to have gone, to "listen," with nothing to say or ask. And after an hour we were out in the hall again, watching the rain pour down from the inky purple sky in infinite regiments, and he took his bicycle and disappeared to the right, and I ran out across the streaming, gritty court and down Downing Street, and through the market. I went on running after the rain had stopped, out of excitement. Because what I had "listened to," what I had "heard," was a mode of being that would allow me to know everything, to feel everything, to use all my faculties, without that fear of being radically inadequate or clumsy that every other available mode imposes. A mode of being for *me* at last; not because of *my* personal peculiarities, but because of my nation and my generation, my intelligence and critical sense, because I am trying to think and feel in England in 1958.

There are many ways to be British, many national types, and the dominant one, the Establishment type, the gentleman, has outlived its usefulness. So much I want to take for granted. I think this is what Orwell meant by saying that England is a family with the wrong members in control, and what puts the pungency of truth into much of Amis's comedy. In any case I want to assume it in order to pass on and define another national type, *the* British type today, as it seems to me.

A national type is something vaguer than a type as we usually understand it, shallower than a mode of being, but more important and powerful than both, culturally. A gentleman can be good or bad, stupid or brilliant, irritable or good-tempered. Gentlemanliness is merely an idea—a syndrome of ideas—in the minds of many widely different individuals. But it is an idea that controls their sensibilities. A gentleman must (so far as he is one) regard certain relations between a man and a woman as ridiculous, others as unnatural, others as distasteful; relations which to a nongentleman can be interesting, exciting, moving. Almost any contemporary account of D. H. Lawrence and his marriage will give you examples of this. The same is true of relations between a colonel and a private, or between an undergraduate and a tobacconist's daughter. This last suggests, of course, the characterizing extremes, which only the stupidest now profess; more intelligent gentlemen have variants of all these predispositions, nearly always ironical, quite often antithetical; they do not cease to be gentlemen for that, they merely become feebler as persons, their opinions unrelated to their sensibilities, unless they root out the old idea, reject it, replace it with a new way of feeling. And the only effective alternative seems to me the one I am about to propose.

When an idea is in its prime its adherents can be ironical or antithetical about it without losing any essential energy. Stalky and Company based their personalities on an antithesis of *St. Winifred's* and *Eric, or Little by Little,* but they embodied the same virtues quite fiercely, merely in a more sophisticated form. Nowadays those virtues are never fierce, in either their simple or their ironical forms. As an example of the gentlemanly mode in full simplicity today I would cite A. L. Rowse, whose vision of England in, for instance, his introduction to Kilvert's *Diaries,* is unreal to the point of pathos.

It is the quintessence of England and the English attitude to life. . . . It is a world of rural deans, and tea on rectory lawns under the trees, and, after tea, archery or croquet, or picking flowers in the flowery meads of Wiltshire for decorating the church, of pretty Victorian girls looking over the parapet of the bridge while the river flows by.

It is hard to realize that that was written after the Second World War. Typical of the gentleman-keeping-up-with-the-times is Christopher Hollis's book on Orwell, which, while arguing that Orwell didn't *have* to hate Crossgates that much, and that what he said about Eton and Burma and the ruling class and left-wing politicians, etc., was really rather exaggerated, has to begin and end by assuming that he told more of the truth than anyone else—that he was the Conscience of his Generation, you know. Or Harold Nicolson's *Journey to Java,* where he describes himself, in terms that recall—perhaps deliberately—*Look Back in Anger,* as a "typical Englishman of the upper income group; well advanced in age, rubicund and stout; slightly ruffled about the hair and collar and therefore probably an intellectual." And Nicolson reflects that that latest phenomenon, the Angry Young Man, "sees in me a well-fed,

plump, flabby, complacent survival from Victorian England."
His defense is quite consciously feeble—"I really do regard
self-satisfaction as a stupid and hampering defect." Contemporary facts demand from men of this type opinions and sympathies, and ultimately actions, which are unnatural to their
sensibilities. Such a type, then, has outlived its usefulness.

The new type I should call the decent man—as opposed to
the gentleman—or the Anglo-Saxon moralist, or the Anglo-
Saxon rebel. In this century all the most central and vital examples have been essentially rebellious, but in the past, and
perhaps in the future, that may turn out to be a secondary
characteristic, that varies with the individual. What is always
essential is its puritanism, taking that to mean a concern with
right and wrong so keen as to set the tone of the whole personality, an eagerness to draw sharp, exclusive lines, mapping out
as much as possible of the world, a distrust of all connoisseur-
ship in experience, all aestheticism. There is also something
lower middle class about this type; it never aims at elegance
or magnificence of the aristocratic kind, or Bohemian irresponsibility or indecent exposure, or ruthless theorizing; always at decency, marriage, domesticity, filial and parental
duties. It is middle-brow; concerned with every subtlety and
profundity of truth, but rendering them plainly, relating
them always to the great moral imperatives, hostile to all
priesthoods and parties and technocracies and esoteric systems.
It is all-round responsible, to class, country, civilization, the
four-square citizen and human being, self-exempted from
nothing, even by genius. The typical movement of its mind is
scrupulous, in bad ways as well as good, and therefore irritable
as well as honorable.

The four examples, the four men who embody most vitally
this idea of England and Englishness, are D. H. Lawrence, F. R.
Leavis, George Orwell, and Kingsley Amis. These men differ
widely in some ways—they embody this idea in different manners, and they are each much more than just the embodiment

99

of it, of course. In Lawrence it is less the novels than the essays, less the works, as a whole, than the man, that concerns us. In Amis it is essentially the novelist's persona, the voice he creates for himself to deal with the facts of his fictional world. In Orwell and Leavis we are not interested in the political and critical principles, or even practice, but in their so vivid personalities, their general mode of dealing with problems of knowledge and feeling and action and being.

To bring the four together in a preliminary way, I would say that when Orwell dismissed the British intelligentsia either as Europeanized, as in *England, Your England,* or as out of date and out of touch, as in the figure of Porteous in *Coming Up for Air,* he was only saying what Amis rendered in fictional terms in the Welch family of *Lucky Jim,* and what Lawrence said after his famous visit to Cambridge during the war; and that all three would have made a significant exception for Leavis, and that he is the only really significant exception they would have made.

Again, the differentness, the antagonism, which exists between this type and the gentleman is obvious in all four cases. Amis's heroes are ill at ease in the educated world to which society calls them as to its highest reward; Jim Dixon and John Lewis reject the basic idea of being a gentleman, and consequently are themselves rejected in turn. Orwell's Flory in *Burmese Days* and Comstock in *Keep the Aspidistra Flying* are in a similar position, unable even to be fair, aggressive against the gentlemanly world to which they refuse to belong. Leavis's whole life at Cambridge has been a parable of this antagonism, and about Lawrence we may take David Garnett's word. "He was the type who provokes the most violent class-hatred in this country; the impotent hatred of the upper classes for the lower."

It will be granted that Leavis is a puritan in the sense I have described, but he may be objected to as high-brow rather than middle-brow, because of his enthusiasm for Eliot and James, his recommendation of Bottrall and Empson, his overvaluation of Conrad and Hawthorne and other writers with interesting "ideas." But it is the temper and tone of his mind, its "personality," more than the particular preferences, that we are interested in. Leavis is the plain man among the critics; to avoid so obvious a comparison as the American New Critics, put him even beside Reuben Brower, and surely he strikes us as not professional. He *is* professional, of course, but the intensity of his impact lifts him out of that classification. He is talking to us too urgently and personally, too *morally,* for that. His best criticism has the character of a sermon. Side by side with the New Critics he seems ignominiously unintellectual. He does not draw striking parallels between different arts and different disciplines. He does not reveal, however discreetly, recondite readings in philosophy and theology. He does not throw out hints of relationships between D. H. Lawrence and St. Augustine, or Crashaw and Polish Baroque, or whatever. He has nothing to say about the nature of knowledge or the language of poetry. All he talks about is English literature and which things in it are better and why. And his standards in judging those things have no metaphysical or theological basis. He judges things by whether they feel right to him. Instead of extending himself in systems and theories until everything can be held in his net and assigned a logical place, as nearly everyone else does, Leavis reduces himself to the residual essence of his experience, moral, social, sexual, intellectual, the single naked unprotected pulse, and records the reaction of that complex of nerves, so endlessly self-purging, to the play, poem, metaphor, opinion, etc.

Side by side with Lionel Trilling and Edmund Wilson, Leavis's personality is less that of the general thinker. He does not present himself as essentially a learned or a brilliant man. He does not make you feel there is a lot to be *known* before you yourself can begin to criticize. Critics like Trilling and Wilson refer you out to politics, economics, psychiatry; critics like Ransom and Tate wield "techniques," precision tools of the intellect. Leavis uses only his own experience. Wherever it came from, it is now only experience; however he uses it is merely a function of the individual situation.

This, then, is the meaning we are giving to "middle-brow" in the essay; thought and expression in which the urgency of meaning fuses the technique into transparency. In James and Eliot, in *Ulysses* and *The Magic Mountain* and *Remembrance of Things Past,* in Faulkner and Dos Passos, the technique claims our interest importantly, independently. *Women in Love* has a markedly original structure, and cannot be read like an ordinary novel; but when you *can* read it, you find the structure transparent, unnoticeable. This is not true of *The Waste Land* or *The Sound and the Fury.* These are high-brow works, where there is a "difficult" intellectual interest, either in the subjects discussed or in the mode of discussion; and in low-brow works there is an anti-intellectual interest. It may be objected that Amis, since we are considering specifically the persona he projects in his novels, should be called low-brow, because of his insistence on jazz, beer, and blondes, his aversion from culture. But even within a projected persona there is room for a difference between what one is and what one says one is. When the Amis figure says he doesn't want culture he merely records a dissatisfaction with its contemporary form; a dissatisfaction that springs from an acute cultural conscience. His heroes are essentially educated men; they merely prefer their manhood to their education when, as they feel, they are forced to choose. (Orwell, as a matter of fact, does project a low-brow persona in *Coming Up for Air.* This is not the side of him that interests us here.) Middle-brow, then, is more a matter of the mode of taste than of its object; it is more an evaluative, less a comparative, term than the other two; Frieda said of Lawrence that he was neither high-brow nor low-brow, he simply "found the living quality in everything."

About the side of Orwell that does concern us Trilling has

made all these same points in his introduction to *Homage to Catalonia*. Orwell has shown us how one can stand

fronting the world with nothing more than one's simple, direct, undeceived intelligence, and a respect for the powers one does have and the work one undertakes to do. . . . He liberates us. He tells us that we can understand our political and social life merely by looking around us, he frees us from the need for the inside dope. He implies that our job is not to be intellectual, certainly not to be intellectual in this fashion or that, but merely to be intelligent according to our lights—he restores the old sense of the democracy of the mind, releasing us from the belief that the mind can work only a technical, professional way, and that it must work competitively. He has the effect of making us believe that we may become full members of the society of thinking men.

This release, this liberation, is part of what I felt after my interview with Leavis.

2. D. H. Lawrence

But you don't catch me going back on my whiteness and Englishness and myself. English in the teeth of all the world, even in the teeth of England . . . I really think that the most living clue of life is in us Englishmen in England, and the great mistake we make is in not uniting together in the strength of this real living clue—religious in the most vital sense—uniting together in England and so carrying the vital spark through.

—*Letters of D. H. Lawrence*

Then beyond class there was the difference in race, to cross over to each other. He, the Englishman, Puritan, stern and uncompromising, so highly conscious and responsible; I, the German, with my vagueness and uncertainty, drifting along . . . Then when Lloyd George came to power Lawrence lost all hope in the spirit of his native country. Lloyd George, who was so un-English, to stand for English prestige! It seemed incredible. . . . Just as it was said of him that he wasn't patriotic; he who seemed to me England itself, a flower sprung out of its most delicate, courageous tradition, not the little bourgeois England but the old England of Palmerstone, whom he admired, when men were still men and not mere social beings."

—Not I but the Wind, FRIEDA LAWRENCE

When I got to the right station, I did not need to linger, while the embracing Germans cleared away, to recognize Lawrence. He did look fearfully English. . . . His hair was of a colour, and grew in a particular way, which I have never seen except in English working men. It was bright mud-colour, with a streak of red in it, a thick mat, parted on one side. Somehow, it was incredibly plebeian, mongrel and underbred. His forehead was broad, but not high, his nose too short and lumpy, his face colourless, like a red-haired man's, his chin (he had not then grown a beard) altogether too large, and round like a hairpin—rather a Philip IV sort of chin—and the lower lip, rather red and moist under the scrubby toothbrush moustache. He looked like a mongrel terrier among a crowd of Pomeranians and Alsatians, English to the bone. He was the type of plumber's mate who goes back to fetch his tools. . . . He was the type who provokes the most violent class-hatred in this country; the impotent hatred of the upper classes for the lower. Certainly Lawrence had no need to carry the Union Jack.

—DAVID GARNETT

Lawrence's puritanism, as much as Leavis's, will pass unchallenged. Even during his lifetime educated criticism blamed him for excess of message and morality, not lack of it. And there is no temptation to call him high-brow or low-brow. But someone may object to his being called lower middle class. It is true that the struggle between his mother and his father was in some ways one of the working class against the lower middle class; and that struggle persisted inside him far too importantly for him to be described as either one, taken in distinction from the other. But there is a sense in which there is only one important class division today, that between the lower middle class, which is taken to subsume the working class, and the upper middle class, subsuming the aristocracy or upper class.

As has been often pointed out, there is no working-class mind in Britain, never has been, and no aristocratic mind nowadays. When a working-class man *thinks,* he does so with no difficulty of transition, in a lower-middle-class mode. Ways of thinking and talking about general problems, if they can be labeled proletarian or aristocratic, are inevitably limited by their labels, made extraordinary, not for serious consideration. But there is an upper-middle-class way of looking at things which enlists the most brilliant talents, Waugh, Greene, Auden, Eliot, etc., and commands the deepest respect. It is in this sense that I am using the term "lower middle class."

The difference between the two is as well defined as anywhere in their respective attitudes toward servants. The lower-middle-class family is most likely, perhaps, to have no servants, and to be uneasy with them, even with waiters and taxi drivers, etc. (See *I Like It Here.*) If there are servants in their houses, they most likely come in by the day, as the Lawrences' did; and they certainly remain fully equal beings, and don't become a different race, as they do in Eliot—"What the fairies do, and what the servants say"—and in Mann—"Disorder and Early Sorrow." The upper-middle-class mind can certainly sympathize fully with servants, as Proust shows, but it has to remove the individual from the category "servant" in order not to find adult emotions in him absurd. For Shaw the manservant who talks ideas is funny; of course, he realizes it shouldn't be; but to him it is. To a lower-middle-class mind it isn't, because he hasn't any category "servant"; and when he comes across the servant mind, with its pliable loyalties, fawnings, and cheatings, he finds it dishonorable, and distasteful, and difficult to sympathize with—more difficult than Proust found it.

Of course, very few people have servants living in now; but that merely means that there is a gap, an absence, in the lives of upper-middle-class people, whatever their incomes; and it is an important reason why the other mind is more suited to today's conditions.

Having no servants, the lower-middle-class man has much more naked contact with work of all kinds, with physical fatigue and danger, with discomfort and humiliation by authority of all kinds. (Compare Lawrence's and Orwell's lives with James's and Eliot's; or see Amis's remarks on this subject in *I Like It Here.*) He travels third class, never first; he is a private soldier, not an officer. (Of course, national service makes everyone a private; but the upper-middle-class boy takes his whole conscript experience as fantasy, as fiction, as Evelyn Waugh.) He lives on what he earns; not on inherited income, or an allowance, or credit, or loans, or theft, or unpaid debts.

Obviously the class quality I am speaking of is a matter of sympathies, not of birth or education. Leavis and Orwell belong fairly clearly to the other class, on those terms. But Trilling, in the essay already quoted, has pointed out how Orwell admired the virtues of the lower middle class, possessions, marriage, fatherhood, and decency. And the climax of *Keep the Aspidistra Flying,* the point that pivots and swings round the hero's whole life, is an epiphany of those values.

The lower-middle-class people in there, behind their lace curtains, with their children and their scraps of furniture and their aspidistras—they lived by the money code, sure enough, and yet they contrived to keep their decency. The money code as they interpreted it was not merely cynical and hoggish. They had their standards, their inviolable points of honour. They "kept themselves respectable"—kept the aspidistra flying. Besides, they were *alive.* They were bound up in the bundle of life. They begot children, which is what the saints and the soul-savers never by any chance do.

Trilling says we are "shocked and dismayed . . . when Orwell speaks out in praise of such things as responsibility, order in personal life, fair play, physical courage . . . the love of personal privacy, of order, of manners, the ideal of fairness and responsibility." Why should we be shocked and dismayed? Only because our consciences and our sensibilities, American as well as British, have been so long directed by nondecent men, left-wing theorists, hairy-chest-beaters, the perverse and doomed, sophisticates and romantics of all kinds. It is only decent men like Orwell who can restore to these qualities their wholly natural glamour, a glamour which is valid under the keenest scrutiny.

Domesticity is something more difficult to demonstrate, but put beside Eliot, Faulkner, Proust, Mann, surely the work of the four we are discussing demonstrates a faith in, an intensity of interest in, marriage, that unites them and marks them off as a group. *The Rainbow* and *Women in Love* are the two greatest modern celebrations of marriage. *That Uncertain Feeling* and *Keep the Aspidistra Flying,* on a lower level, both end with affirmations of marriage that are amazing in the face of the difficulties and disadvantages they have explored. Let us compare them, not with *The Cocktail Party* or *The Heart of the Matter,* but with Proust's treatment of the Odette-Swann relationship, or that between Albertine and the narrator. Proust is obviously the greater writer, who tells us far more about his characters and their relationship. But that relationship is not marriage. It is one of the varieties of love. It hasn't the permanence, the propriety, the communality, the conjugality, of marriage. It is just the difference between, say, Lawrence and Colette. Chéri and Edmée, after ten years of mutual maneuvering, sexual, sentimental, and financial, have no idea of that marriage which Paul and Miriam, Paul and Clara, from the first strain toward, approximate themselves to, cannot do without. Nor do I see that idea in *Brideshead Revisited, The Horse's Mouth,* or *Mrs. Dalloway.* Or in Faulkner, Hemingway, or Dos Passos. There are other ideas—*characterizations*—of marriage, in some of them, but none with the quality of vision, no celebrations.

There is no intrinsic reason, of course, why this idea of marriage is to be preferred in art. In other circumstances, in another generation, it may be just the mark of the commonplace, the vulgar, the dead-alive, to embody this idea in a novel. It is important now because it is one mark of decency, and decency is now "the most living clue of life."

Decency means cleanliness, in the most literal sense—"It means kindling the life-quality where it was not. Even if it's only in the whiteness of a washed pocket-handkerchief." The difference between dirt and cleanness, order and disorder, dust and neatness, is an obsession in *Homage to Catalonia* and in *That Uncertain Feeling*. It means practicalness—"He could cook, he could sew, he could darn a stocking and milk a cow, he was an efficient wood-cutter and a good hand at embroidery, fires always burned when he had laid them and a floor, after Lawrence had scrubbed it, was thoroughly clean." It means plainness; moth-eaten red plush has no glamour for it; nor even new red plush. It means ordinariness, in a sense that can include Lawrence, but would exclude even Yeats. It means directness, in which irony and ambiguity and image and mask will be subordinate. It means personalness, the quality that makes every judgment of Leavis's (and of the others) so much a self-commitment and self-exposure, that has made him the only immature person to attend the university of Cambridge in the last forty years.

And consequently it does not mean elegance or eloquence or brilliance or civilization or ripeness. It *will* mean them; once it can establish its hegemony, extend itself, stop fighting for its life. At the moment its exponents can only afford their primary virtues. But they embody those virtues in a really primary, really vigorous sense. Not in the sense in which Colette's biographers, for instance, can call her provincial, naïve, countrified, honorable, and modest. All these things are true—and highly admirable—but only paradoxically; when you have taken it for granted that she was far more highly sophisticated, urban, and amoral. Just as Henry James's enthusiasts can describe him as Rabelaisian in his gusto for words. The paradoxical truth about the decent men—and exhilarating truth it is—is that they are subtle, learned, brilliant, highly civilized, and gentlemen to their finger tips.

My contention, at any rate, is that Englishmen must accord these qualities and these men a primary place in their imaginative lives. It is a valuable American insight into British culture that we have a habit of creating figures which simultaneously represent and inspire us. In this same essay of Trilling's he remarks that Orwell was such a figure, and as such was an essentially British phenomenon. America, he says, has no such figures. Edmund Wilson, too, in his most recent article on T. S. Eliot, in *The New Yorker,* claims that for Englishmen Eliot is a "figurehead," and comments at length on our need to erect these, and to bow down to them. Such figures are to be found at all levels of a culture, and the quality of a man's life is largely determined by the figure he chooses, the figures he finds to choose from, and the manner and the degree (neither of them wholly his responsibility) in which he responds to it when chosen. For Americans, at least, it is our middle-brow figures who are the really interesting and potent ones, according to Richard Chase. He says there is in America a "provincial, anti-intellectual, protestant moralism which finds its comic self-awareness in writers like Kingsley Amis, its literary-critical champion in F. R. Leavis, and its prophetic voice in D. H. Lawrence. Which is to say that, as always, American middle-browism feels more strongly drawn to English than to American, French, or Russian writers." (Obviously, for Mr. Chase middle-brow covers more than it does for me; it covers most, in fact, of what I mean by decent.) Mr. Chase's remark is a very valuable hint of the way Britain can retain some importance and self-respect in her new world situation. But even more important, in order to live at all, Britain must make sure that her figures have some power for her young people, that they can recognize themselves in that reflection, and are excited by this image of achieved life. If not, if the figures are alien, or outworn, or images of defeat—and I think that ours are now—then young people with imagination will not throw themselves forward into life, into the great enterprises and adventures; they will merely look after themselves, avoid trouble.

The anecdote I tell below illustrates some of this. For though the officer and the sergeant were too young and callow to be very effective figures at best, they had it in their power, because of their intelligence, their education, their official rank, their official opportunity, to in some degree explain the world to the rest of us, to show us how to deal with it. They had even the abortive desire to. They failed, far worse than failed, because *they* had modeled *themselves* after the wrong images, images of moral and spiritual bankruptcy. And what better had society offered them, in their brilliant careers of scholarships and examinations? How often had the image of decency been recommended to them, however implicitly, by their teachers and writers? And yet someone modeled on that image could have begun, in even an hour, to get through to that audience.

Decency is the most living clue of life because it could enable our leaders to form themselves in an image that would genuinely arouse us, that we could respond to with enthusiasm. There has been no enthusiasm in England for a long time. But there could be. I could care about politics. And politics is only typical. The same is true of all forms of leadership and discipleship. The connection between men is less electric than it used to be, the instinctive leaping forward into a belief or a cause much feebler—feebler than it is in the U.S.A., for example. Because the forms life takes, the face it presents to us, is faded, worn, dejected. It has no vigor, and calls forth none in us. That is why no one is interested in party politics, why no one will buy a literary magazine, and personal security and advancement are the only effective motives.

3. Hegemony

After Cambridge I did my national service—that prolonged submersion in systematized anarchy by which we all come of age these days. There we were, thirty huts with forty men in each, and the Light Programme on full blast, jumping to stiff and quivering attention whenever one of our nineteen year old corporals came into the room. Spending hours every night on our unfirable rifles, our unwearable "parade" boots, the white lumps of coal that lay on top of our scuttles, the knife fork spoon and razor we laid out for daily inspection, and which we never ate or shaved with. And after inspection we were assembled to hear our corporals demonstrate how to seduce a woman, and how to bring about an abortion; and everything, in what they did, and in how we could at all react to it, was destruction—hatred, violation, resentment, boredom, destruction.

The boys in my flight were all from round Derby, a warm-voiced, affectionate, sceptical lot, very naïve and very sophisticated. I remember Len telling us the embarrassment of his younger brother (how old could *he* be?) getting up one Sunday morning to find his best suit stained with blood; he'd taken his belt off to his girl-friend the night before, to keep her in line a bit, and in the darkness he hadn't noticed what he was doing to his suit. He had to keep his mother out of the bedroom all day. But Len was cheerful, indifferent, unbullyable, decent. George, on the other hand, was baby-faced, bespectacled, round-shouldered and dirty-minded, but a wonderful sentimental-malicious humorist. He used to imitate our corporals and officers marvellously, standing on the table in the middle of the hut; and even did a kind of literary parody, of how the Lady Ermyntrude, in her velvet gown, gazed through her brocaded curtains out at the gathering dusk, and murmured, huskily, "Well fuck me, it's pissing down."

We all went for an hour a week to hear an education lecture on current events and one week it was on "The Third World War." There were over a thousand of us in the camp cinema-cum-church, when the Education Officer and his sergeant, both of them just down from Oxford, strolled along the aisle and up on to the platform, and sat rocking their chairs back, ankle on knee, chatting to each other. They were both growing little moustaches, but the officer was lanky and fair and physically blank, the other broad-shouldered and handsome, with wavy black hair. Then the officer introduced the lecture, in his light, toneless, whimsical, trailing voice, that could only come to life at moments of cynicism. And Sgt. Hunter, who had the richest, roundest, most modulated, most unreal voice, told us when the next war might come, and whom we would be fighting, and how many of us would be killed, and what slim chances there were of not using the bomb, and how many and how each bomb would kill. It was a gesture, of course; though sincere—this was the only way he knew how to "think"; but such thoughts were as unreal in him as his voice. He was a literary ladies' Don Juan, with his warm blue eyes, warm mouth, and high colour under his freckles. You might have thought the whole thing was suggested by the officer, except that he never made suggestions, much less gestures; he was as recessive and tactical as the other was "brilliant." The lecture over, they descended from the platform and passed up the aisle chatting to each other, the officer sniggering, oblivious of all us, sitting at attention.

Afterwards of course George gave us the whole thing again in our hut. And he brought out, in his way, all the essential things, the affectation, the isolation, the ineffectuality, the insolence, the imposter-quality. Len said, "Well, Christ, I'd get those two buggars before any bloody hydrogen bomb got me. I'd get those two with my little old pen-knife." And George replied, in Hunter's voice, "Why, Leonard, we aren't going to be there. We're what you're bloody well fighting for."

A family with the wrong members in control—that, perhaps, is as near as one can come to describing England in a phrase.
                                    —ORWELL, *England, Your England*

It may be objected that I am proposing a dictatorship; a narrow and exclusive dominance by a temperament congenitally narrow and exclusive. Are all our books and films, our minds, to work along the same lines, dealing with the same things in the same ways? No, all that is in question is a hegemony, something which has always existed, and which already exists at this moment. Only insofar as there is a dictatorship at present, of gentlemanliness, should there be one in the future. In fact, it should be less dictatorial, the new hegemony; the old one is suffering from rigor mortis.

A hegemony is a dynamic hierarchy of images, which imposes on the individual mind an order of preference and reverence and expectation. So that there is no sense of opposition, rather of positive harmony, between the different images, the different ways to be, only one will always want to be A rather than B, the gentleman rather than the loyal servant, except insofar as one feels oneself personally limited, or insofar as one rebels. And one will always identify more wholly, in the imagination, take orders more easily, in practical life, from A, the dominant type, the gentleman. And will always expect certain things from certain types, according to the hegemony; romantic love, for instance, from the gentleman, comic discontent from the Cockney.

This would mean that if the decent men became the dominant image, those of us of indeterminate type, the Herbert Pockets and Hastings, would choose our Pips and our Marlowes, political and religious as well as personal, from among the most vigorous and shrewd, most straightforward and masculine of the men we know. Really aristocratic natures would continue to function as such, and would fulfill themselves exactly as before, only out of the spotlight.

The hegemony of gentlemanliness has meant that we have tended to give our keenest sympathy and participation to the sensitive, distinguished, amoral, elegant, and maladjusted. It has meant that for the last thirty years, at least, since the dominant type started losing its vitality. And though in practical life, of course, employers cannot prefer this type, most culturally important appointments are not really a part of practical life, and those that are go to men who combine with this social and imaginative weary grace an unrelated, unexpected, ruthless efficiency in administration. In dislocated personalities of this kind the will develops enormously. The officer of my anecdote is an example. Even in military life this type is trusted and preferred above others; this is much more true in the world of the imagination.

This direction of sympathy is seen clearly in the work of Evelyn Waugh and Graham Greene, two writers who have struck the most contemporary of notes. Basil Seal and Ambrose Silk, however useless and absurd and immoral Waugh may show them to be, are the ones out of the whole range of his characters which retain his sympathy and delight to the end—and, while we are under his influence, our sympathy and delight. In *England Made Me* Greene's most vivid and, in the novel's terms, engaging characters are both failed gentlemen, haunted by the ideal they have betrayed, and with nothing to recommend them but that ghost. Simpler presentations of the gentleman-hero, by perhaps subtler minds, are to be found in Virginia Woolf, and Elizabeth Bowen, and twenty others. In all these the nongentlemanly figures are thin, unconvincing, caricatural; for example, the lower-class characters in *Death of the Heart,* the barmaid in *Brighton Rock,* the Cockney in Waugh's *Work Suspended*. But even where the lower-class types are well done, they can take only subordinate parts, exhibit subordinate virtues, be "characters." Take, for example, Stanley Holloway's Doolittle in *My Fair Lady*. A hero has to be gentlemanly, even against all probability; in Carol Reed's *A Kid for Two Farthings,* a realistic film of East End life, the little boy who was the central character was manifestly upper-class, in manners, accent, intonation, haircut, everything. Or take panoramic films like *In Which We Serve,* where every social type is given its place, its kind and intensity of virtue, of dignity, of philosophy, of love, and they mount one above another to a pinnacle of gentlemanliness. This is the hegemony in action.

This hierarchy, this dictatorship, is moreover getting stronger, not weaker. During the last thirty or forty years, the alternatives, the ways of being different, which every normal cultural system allows, have in England gotten fewer and feebler. People have conformed more and more closely to the dominant pattern.

There are, of course, contemporary writers who have never celebrated the gentleman ideal; the work of some of them expresses even a lower-middle-class sensibility. For example, at different levels, J. B. Priestley, Winifred Holtby, C. P. Snow. But these writers offer no effective challenge to the *status quo,* the hegemony. Why is that? What makes them so much less interesting than the four I am discussing?

It is striking in them all that though they have dealt with contemporary materials and contemporary problems far more conscientiously than, say, the four novelists last mentioned, they have had far less effect on the modern sensibility. And this is no accidental injustice. They are out of date. They have none of them met the challenge of specifically modern life, that is, of the First World War. It is, after all, from the experience of 1917, either directly of the fighting, or indirectly of the collapse of "social" morality, that all of modern American literature begins, Eliot, Cummings, Dos Passos, Hemingway, Fitzgerald, Faulkner. New forms of lyric and narrative verse, new forms of the short story and novel, new criticism, all were developed to express the new sensibility. In England the response was slower and less generous, but in Eliot and Huxley, Auden, Isherwood, Greene, Waugh, gradually new forms of characterization, incident, structure, tone, etc., etc., evolved. But they were all upper middle class. The lower-middle-class mind continued to discuss its experience exactly as it had before, to acknowledge as experience only those kinds of things that would fit into the old categories. Priestley, Snow, Winifred Holtby continued to produce characters and incidents, panoramic constructions and final consummations, just like those Wells wore out before 1914, those Lawrence turned his back on in *The Rainbow*. Snow, for instance, continues to build his serious characters out of contrasting layers—the absurdly vain and ineffectual and yet shrewd, the histrionic and emotionally dishonest and yet sincere—and to borrow his comic ones from Dickens. Virginia Woolf, Elizabeth Bowen, a dozen novelists from the upper middle class, turned away from all that, and constructed new forms for themselves. They had James for a model; but then the lower-middle-class had Lawrence, if anyone had explained him. But the explainers were all in the other camp—see Eliot's remarks on James and on Lawrence—and the blind led the blind into a circular standstill, a pointless marktime far from the main road. The lower-middle-class mind lost all contemporaneity, ceased to be exciting. The hegemony became a narrower, stiffer thing, including fewer alternatives, imposing stricter discipline.

An example of this is Winifred's Holtby's *Mandoa, Mandoa,* which is in intention a left-wing *Black Mischief,* written a year or two after Waugh's book came out; which fails not so much because she was less talented than he as because his sensibility and his form were incorruptibly one, and his sensibility was incorruptibly upper middle class. You can't put lower-class sympathies into that kind of book. And her *South Riding,* a respectable piece of work, built entirely on "decent" values, with two categorically lower-middle-class heroines, a schoolmistress and a woman alderman, is topped off with a romantic, reactionary, wounded, brooding, ineffectual, upper-middle-class hero. The hegemony was too much for her. For a hero she had to have a gentleman. Because *her* sensibility, *her* themes, had no contemporary forms. (The *Old Wives' Tale,* before the war, had not needed to do that.) The same is true of Priestley in, for instance, *The Good Companions* and *The Linden Tree.* The hero is refined and sensitive and not quite tough enough for this world; and of another sensibility from the rest of the work. Snow avoids this trap, being a much more intelligent writer, but his Lewis Eliot never becomes a really effective hero; because he focuses a precontemporary mind. (I try to justify this more below.) Snow's novels remain a considerable achievement, but without the excitement and potency of contemporary statement. All the lower-middle-class writers were, as it were, out of time and out of touch.

(E. M. Forster is an example of an upper-middle-class mind failing to meet the challenge of modern times. *Passage to India* is "out of time"; does it take place before or after the Great War? Surely no other intelligent book published in 1924—and so concerned with the modern mind—so completely ignores what had just happened to the world. This was, of course, a good deal the result of his virtues. The way the upper-middle-class mind faced the modern world was not attractive. He was right to refuse to take up the defensive reactionary posture that Eliot, etc., made fashionable, to remain a liberal, to remain "interested in political and social problems." But consequently, despite his magnificent talents, his work is sterile and he himself has found it almost impossible to write. He has been, in the same essential sense as Snow, Priestley, Holtby, out of touch.)

Before specifically modern times, then, there was much more flexibility and vigor, change and life, in the hegemony, and writers like Wells and Bennett and Gissing and Hardy and Lawrence could project their lower-middle-class personae quite unashamedly, and quite contemporarily; and upper-middle-class writers like Forster could be in sympathy with them. But things have rigidified since then, in every way. Snow comments on this, from his own point of view, in *Homecoming*. When the hero—Lewis Eliot—was young, all his friends had assumed that social barriers were shrinking, loosening, snapping, day by day, and that perhaps even in their lifetimes people would relate themselves to each other purely according to their native talents and tastes and capacities for joy. They all worked to promote this end, with a political, economic, social understanding provided most typically by Shaw and Wells. But now (the novel takes place in 1948) he realized that the opposite had happened; socially, educationally, artistically, administratively, (and Snow knows those categories) the prescribed forms are more sharply defined, more ruthlessly insisted on. And his friends, and most able intelligent men he knows, no longer expect, no longer want, that expansion and freedom and greater vigor. In other words, their imaginations have withered and died under the clamp of that hierarchy, that dictatorship.

All this is very interesting and convincing and one is grateful to Snow for corroborating one's impressions. But he concludes his passage: "Looking round their wedding party, I could not shake off a cliché of those years, this was the end of an epoch; I should have liked the company of those who could see one beginning." There one begins to disagree with him. For the trouble is that he was looking for the same kind of "epoch" and "beginning" and "seer" as he had believed in in his youth. The political-economic kind. He had been wrong and out of date then, as Lawrence and Orwell and Leavis were all in their different ways telling him. The essential problems could not be solved that way. How much more out of date today, when the contraction and stiffening, the unhealthy swelling and near-paralysis of the hegemony is so much advanced, so much more noticeable. The most direct equivalents today of his friends of the twenties are not particularly hoping for political and social change, and so perhaps he does not recognize them as "those who see a new epoch beginning." Even those undergraduates who are politically active at contemporary Oxford are interested primarily in *cultural* change.

In "The New Left at Oxford," published in the Manchester *Guardian* last summer, David Marquand writes:

The real significance of the present wave of Left-wing politics is precisely its dissimilarity to that of twenty years ago, both in personnel and ideology. In the thirties the characteristic Oxford revolutionary hailed from an impeccable upper-middle-class background. Communist perorations were, typically, delivered in the cut-glass accents of the English public schools. Today the rebels are more often from the working or lower middle class, products of the Welfare State revolution which reached Oxford after 1945. This has given their political position an extra bite. Their predecessors of twenty years ago might condemn society on intellectual grounds, but they accepted its traditional institutions emotionally. . . . But it does at least say something new—its second great difference from the Left in Oxford in the thirties. For in the thirties Oxford politics reflected politics outside. Oxford feared what everyone feared: unemployment, fascism, war. Now Oxford Socialists usually reject the preoccupations of professional politicians. . . . Indeed they are scarcely concerned at all with politics as usually understood. What are they concerned with instead? The short, superficial answer is, culture. *"Look Back in Anger,"* one prominent university Left-winger shouted at me recently, his voice almost shaking with passion, "is a more important political document than anything the Labour party has said since 1951.". . . . Culture and politics are bound together; politics is about people, not the economic men of the laissez-faire textbooks. And in the end people's values, and the terms of reference within which they live—politically too—are set by the films they see and the newspapers they read, not the speeches their M.P. delivers to a half empty House of Commons.

These people do not perhaps "see a new epoch beginning," but they see the old one ending with the same relief and excitement and energetic impatience with which Snow and his friends watched the end of Edwardianism. And they have a new idea, a new direction to go in; which defines itself, as new directions always do, by its opposition to the old one; it is *not* political or economic change, but cultural renewal. These are the people Snow was looking for; he did not recognize them because they were not saying what he expected. But it is exactly what Lawrence, Leavis, Orwell, and Amis have long expected them to say. They have been teaching Englishmen to ask those questions for many years now, and they have been enacting the answers in their own lives.

(Some of the reasons for that change of interest can be found in G. D. H. Cole's *Condition of Britain*, of 1957. Between 1939 and 1954 the population rose, despite the war, by 6.5 per cent. Consumption rose 12 per cent, and was far more equally distributed. All these facts go directly against the predictions of the thirties, and discredit the whole climate of prophecy that relied on them. In Seebohm Rowntree's studies of poverty in York, in 1936 there were seventeen thousand below the poverty line, in 1951 there were seventeen hundred. Those numbers amount to 30 per cent and 2 per cent of the respective working populations. And of those needy cases, in 1936 60 per cent were due to unemployment and inadequate wages; in 1951, under 10 per cent—90 per cent being caused by sickness and old age. Obviously a young man's sense of something continuing rotten in the state is going to have to focus on some other area as the source of the trouble. The political-social remedy, the one Snow advocates, has been applied, has had its chance.)

But whatever the reasons for this change of interest, the consequences are plain. It is the quality of life of the people that will be henceforth of first concern, the quality of their culture, the truthfulness, imaginativeness, generosity, acuteness, of the films they see and newspapers they read. And once you begin to examine English culture with any passionate concern, you are soon brought up against that paralyzed and paralyzing hegemony of gentlemanliness. You realize that some alternative must be found, some other dominant cultural image, to replace the gentleman. And you can only conclude, I think, that the decent man, the Anglo-Saxon moralist, is that other image, that new essential Englishman.

4. Kingsley Amis

He gazed out of the window. London was looking full of good stuff. Admittedly it, together with the rest of the United Kingdom, was the land of Sorry-sir (sorry sir bar's closed sir, sorry sir no change sir, sorry sir too late for lunch sir, sorry sir residents only sir), but one couldn't expect to win all the time. . . . This self-restraint, however, could not alter the essential abroadness of the place, the things it must share with millions of square miles between here and Istanbul. All that sun, which made you set out to be wonderful and colourful instead of keeping quiet and getting on with the job. All that geography and biology, which made you behave as if you had invented the country instead of just living in it. All those buildings, either violently architectural and historical or else token and temporary. All that wasted space. All that air of maturity, lack of nervousness and doubt, devotion to serious shouting argument or dedicated gaiety, naturalness which was always an actor's naturalness. All those revving motor bikes, all those touts, all that staring—which in England would be the mindless inquisitiveness of those whose greyly uniform lives were nourished on mere sensation, but in the sunny South was a frank, free, healthy, open, uninhibited curiosity. . . . Going and standing on the touch-lines of other chaps' ways of life and telling yourself you're joining in isn't very self-aware. Just like going through foreign poetry with a dictionary and telling yourself you're reading it.

—I Like It Here

I thought of that upper-class crowd. Why couldn't they be Welsh, I wondered, or since they were mostly Welsh by birth, why couldn't they stay Welsh? Why had they got to go around pretending to be English all the time?—not that there was anything, or anything very serious, wrong with being English, providing you were it to start with. Those who are Welsh to start with should stick to being it. The examples of old Probert, the nut-faced clergyman, and such minor figures as the woman who'd ticked me off on the bus when I was in traditional national dress, were of service in demonstrating the complementary dangers of being too keen on being Welsh.

Then I thought of what I was going to do. Since I seemed to have piloted myself into the position of being immoral and moral at the same time, the thing was to keep trying to be moral, and then to keep trying might turn into a habit. I was always, at least until I reached the climacteric, going to get pulled two ways, and keeping the pull from going the wrong way, or trying to, would have to take the place, for me, of stability and consistency. Not giving up was the important thing.

I poured the milk into two cups, feeling a bit nervous, because this not-giving-up business, was all very fine and large, but it wouldn't be any good if I tried it on my own, if it only applied to me. That was the one important condition. I took the cups upstairs and into Jean's and my bedroom.

—That Uncertain Feeling

These quotations evoke very inadequately Amis's image of the lower-middle-class, nongentlemanly conscience, the creation of which is his great achievement. With more brilliance and insight and spontaneity, more novelist's talent, than Orwell, he has created a voice, a way of talking about everything, and about oneself as one does so, which contains every tone, every modulation of tone, of that mode of being; the naïvely puritan morality, the subtly scrupulous, almost nagging habit of mind, the suspicion of all pretentiousness and falsity, the cardinal importance given to genuineness, the strenuously unheroic posture, the strongly moral sense of humor, above all the sense of being at home in lower-middle-class England as nowhere else.

Amis has an amazing gift for the detail that distinguishes the gentleman from the decent man, not sociologically, but vitally, magnifying, that is, the decent man into the figure of life and dehumanizing the other into simple nastiness; details of opinion, taste, manners, language, morals, knowledge, everything.

It is not his sense of comedy which seems to be so important, though there are some very funny things in *Lucky Jim*. It is his exact knowledge of just what kind of people the Welches are, just how quick-witted and how stupid, how well-meaning and how malevolent, how liberal and how conservative; and which phrases, which opinions, which tastes, express that. It is his exact rendering of Margaret Peel, how much pity and how much exasperation she provokes, how much of each she deserves. It is even more his creation of a hero, Jim Dixon, who holds our liking and approval and sympathy as normal. And above all it is the beautiful adjustment of the problems to the hero, so that by them we simultaneously discover and recognize him, and the resentments, aspirations, fears, disgusts, energies, they generate in him. We discover and recognize them as true; not only for him, not only for anyone in his situation, but for anyone in England. Margaret Peel is a modern type; we have all had to deal with her, though we scarcely realized it till he described the problem to us. Amis makes us recognize the situations themselves, seeing a significance in them we hadn't seen before, just as we recognize the type of man the hero is as more significant, more centrally healthy and decent, than we had realized before. He and they belong together and symbolize the modern predicament. In other words, he creates an image.

In *That Uncertain Feeling* again it is the exact nature of John Lewis's problems and of his appeal to the reader, which give the book its quality. It is his kind of honesty, his blend of humor and seriousness about himself, his mixture of immoral and sternly moral impulses (seen best in the resolution of his internal conflict over his promotion, and over his marital fidelity); and it is the mixture of the likable and the detestable in Elizabeth Gruffydd Williams, the strong and the weak, the pitiable and the glamorous, which constitute her temptation for him. It is this exquisite moral calculation, expressing itself always in sharp social-cultural details, which is the writer's distinction. And his method is that of the image-maker. The point of each succeeeding episode is to deepen our identification with, and participation in, the central character. Like Salinger, Amis has either a first-person narration or a central character whose vision and idiom dominate every moment of the book. But unlike Salinger, Amis does not ask admiration, or even love, for his heroes; only approval and liking; they have no glamour, they are merely decent. They are not even so importantly believable, so independently alive, as Holden Caulfield or Zooey Glass. The one thing Amis has so far created with some intensity and purity is the voice which he lends to each of them in turn. For the rest, his images are low-powered, but of the finest quality.

I should like, in conclusion, to attempt my own image of the essential Englishman; which is therefore the image of England that I can respond to, recognize myself in, aspire to resemble, that can put a face on life for one born here that excites, arouses, suffuses, dignifies, magnifies. He is small, neat, quick-moving, with a fresh-colored, neat-featured, unemphatic face, without physical stateliness, wheeling a bicycle, carelessly dressed, open-necked, plain-mannered, shrewd, skeptical, friendly-jeering in tone, hostile to all elaborateness or eccentricity, unwilling to talk his emotions, but quick in his sympathies, soon intimately related to you, jealous of his masculinity, a family man, essentially private, needing and creating around him the atmosphere of decency, kindliness, cleanliness; the sort of man who asks skeptical questions after the meeting.

This is an image of the common denominator, with no special talents, virtues, intensities; my four principal subjects show the kinds of glamour proper to the type. But this is the man for whom and about whom Orwell and Amis write, from whom Leavis and Lawrence take their departure, to whom they return, on whose behalf they legislate and prophesy. And unless this image becomes dominant in the hegemony of the British mind, unless our M.P.'s and officers and teachers and novelists and works managers get to be more like this, or at least recognize this, value it, prefer it, serve it, Britain will stop growing, the nut will dry up, shrivel, go rotten, inside the gentlemanly shell.

When I had finished writing "British Decency" I had the strongest feeling that I had been singing somebody else's tune; while I reread I would be half-conscious of the same notes and phrases echoing just behind mine; but when I stopped to listen, I could not hear the original. I could not discover, rummaging through the likely sources in my mind, anyone who had followed a significantly similar pattern.

Anyway, I felt more and more sure of my case. So many things that summer seemed to corroborate and confirm me. I spent some weeks in Cambridge for the first time since I had been an undergraduate there, and it was borne in on me how uniquely theatrical it is. The physical layout itself acts as a burning-glass lens for all the impulses to self-dramatization. The pavements and roadways are, by any modern standard, consciously narrow and twisting and crowded; the paths through the college courts expose you to the stare of three rows of windows on all four sides; the bridges nudge each other fifty yards apart on the comically small river; when you punt—the most self-conscious of sports—you do so under the surveillance of elegants sauntering along the banks and lounging on the bridges. When you do anything in Cambridge you are watched; and by no mixed anonymous crowd; by very intelligent, very self-conscious people between eighteen and twenty-one, all pas-

sionately apprenticed to style and elegance and wit. There could be no more perfect conditions for activating the wrong nerves.

The university seemed a good deal more adjusted to modern conditions than when I had been there—and in better repair, more prosperous, more holiday-minded—but internally even less alive, less meaningful. Just because it is a longer time now since the place was spontaneously in the contemporary rhythm, a longer time that it has been consciously adapting itself to that. It is trying—and one can use it as a microcosm of the country as a whole in this—to adapt itself to the times in external matters, while remaining true to itself and its past in spirit. But that self is not the vigorous form of life that, at its best, Cambridge has achieved from time to time; it is the memory of the past, in which the actual achievements are much less important than the evocative nostalgia that accompanies them. To be true to that self is mere self-blinkering, self-diminishing conservatism. Such a spirit makes all external modernization irrelevant.

The university-approved guide that led the foreign students I was teaching on a tour of the colleges said things like, "This dining hall was built by (say) Henry VIII; but we aren't very proud of him, partly because he cut off the heads of rather a lot of people, some of whom were married to him, and partly because . . ." And though, of course, young men don't talk so much like that, it seems to me that they merely abstain. They don't really reject the possibility; it doesn't deeply offend them. But the next step in British life can only come after taking such offense. For that frail, sweet chord is the key in which all the old deceitful symphonies were played.

I knew now that all these pieces belonged together, had been about the same subject, even though it was only at this point that I realized what the subject was. The best way to describe their relationship, to the subject and to each other, is to call them successive stages in the embryonic development of an

126

idea; assuming, for the moment, the recapitulation theory of the development of the human embryo, the fetus takes on, at successive stages, fairly distinct characteristics of the forms of life which succeeded each other during the evolutionary development of the species; ontogeny recapitulates phylogeny; at one stage, for instance, the human fetus has, in incipient form, the gills and the tail of a fish, and then loses both, and takes on, as a later stage, higher vertebrate, mammalian, but still non-human characteristics, which it loses in turn. So in these essays the idea, the subject, as feeble and primitive in conception as "something wrong with England," took on for a time, for instance, the form of a political idea, that England was undemocratic, at a later time became regional, speaking in terms of North and South. With each new stage, the old form was left behind pretty completely—there was at least no logical addition, of A to B, of brick upon brick—and yet it was the same idea in each formulation, and growing bigger and more vigorous each time. And now the embryo was recognizably human, had taken on its final form. But I had come a long way, with the Lawrence, Leavis, Orwell, and Amis essay, from the concern with America, and with social-political phenomena which had been so marked in the first pieces. Both these concerns, I knew, were still a part of the idea; but in seeking and defining the ultimate, deepest sources of power in England, of Englishness, I had had to neglect them. Now it was time to show that British decency was the beginning of the answer to all the crucial problems of identity and relationship England was facing. England's attitude to America, to the Commonwealth, to her world responsibilities, to herself in her present stage of historical development, must all be reinterpreted in the light of that insight. Sure now of the essential Englishman, I next had to sketch out the essential England, in these larger, less literary terms.

A MIRROR FOR ANGLO-SAXONS

1. What We Have

Looked tough, was tall and permanently bronzed
(I should guess Berkeley, do not quote me, though)
Not an ounce above the statutory weight,
Two hundred pounds, most of it bone and muscle;
Blue-eyed, with jutting chin and jutting brows.
The nose, however, did not command the chin.
Myself, I would rather have no chin at all
Than one that dared be wiser than its boss.
As for his mouth, a man-sized Cupid's bow,
Curved for kissing a diminutive mother
And flashing teen-age smiles of high intent;
Was that the cause, or was it one more symptom,
Of his twin habits—equally repulsive
To us inveterate Western Europeans—
Downing a mid-day pint of raw cow's milk,
And treating France's noblest vintages
Like bath-tub gin whenever he got high.
                —"Superman on the Riviera," ROBERT GRAVES

This poem seems to me an unusually interesting example of
the Englishman's image of the American. Interesting for the
truth in it—test it out on Jeffrey Hunter the film star, one of
America's own idealizations of herself; and for the spite in it
—the language is so impoverished by "personal" feeling that

the poem ends up quite crudely pompous and stupid. The image in itself is familiar: the best-known version is, of course, the Alden Pyle of Graham Greene's *The Quiet American;* a more earnest type, but equally teen-age. The observation there is not keen, and the feeling quite dismissible, but I have discovered that the implied indictment of America seems completely convincing to Englishmen who usually rise above Graham Greene—never mind the regular Greene public, which is after all an impressive segment of intelligent reading England.

The novel, moreover, gives a more vivid picture than the poem of the Englishman who confronts and describes this American. Fowler, the narrator of *The Quiet American,* is even more one of "us inveterate Western Europeans" than Graves; he has built his life completely on a modish despair, glamourized by the habits of opium, *Les Fleurs du Mal,* and a native girl to share his bed each night; he has seen through every illusion and ideal, from marriage to democracy, from truth to love, and is irritated by Pyle's continued faith in them. He says he is fond of Pyle, but what he makes us feel much more is his irritation, condescension, and resentment of him. Between the Englishman and the American, both British writers imply, and practical experience often confirms, these must be the dominant feelings.

Why this should be so was best explained, I think, by A. J. Liebling in his *New Yorker* review of *The Quiet American,* where he commented on the historical parallels that exist for this kind of double image. He pointed out that all the things Greene accused his American of were just what the English themselves have traditionally been accused of by the French; a lack of taste about food and drink, complacent ignorance of other languages and cultures, juvenility and romanticism about sex, a tiresome faith in official sources and eagerness for practical action, altogether too much well-scrubbed, big-shouldered innocence, too little sophistication, skepticism, *savoir-vivre.* He pointed out further that this French image of the Englishman was a feature of the nineteenth century, after Waterloo, when

England unmistakably drew ahead of France in the competition for world power. (It was not unknown, of course, in the eighteenth century; nor was this Graves-Greene image of the American unknown before today; the new situations merely gave these images greater currency and purchasing power, made reserves of national humiliation and resentment generally available to them.) Moreover, the French were subjected to the same ridicule by the Italians in the sixteenth century, when they had gradually welded their country together into unity and independence and efficiency. And the Greeks found the Romans crude, at the time of Rome's greatness. In each case the younger, more vigorous country confessed a great cultural debt, a long cultural tutelage; and the older, beaten country jeered that it had not learned, never would learn, the essential lesson. "Nevertheless, you remain nasty, overgrown children," is Mr. Liebling's phrase.

In other words, the existence of this double image, of the two countries in confrontation, is a symptom of not only a state but a feeling of inferiority, on the part of the older country; a feeling that spawns all kinds of malice and misunderstanding and dislike. Let us cram all these feelings and ideas, for the sake of maneuverability, into a single phrase, and say the British claim that Americans are "immature" and they themselves "mature."

This British attitude is a fact we are all aware of, but don't usually mention in a practical discussion of Anglo-American relations, because we think of it in too crudely moral terms, as envy or jealousy, matters for simple self-correction. But the complex of feelings that finds expression in it is too powerful and persistent, both in this individual case and in the historical pattern exposed above, to be so dismissed; I mean there is too much truth in the observation, too much justification for the hostility, too much subtlety and too much seriousness, to be merely the work of envy. Other powers are also at work here, and they are ready to work more usefully, if we can find the terms to release and redirect them. And this is neither a moral nor a personal matter. An Englishman, a generous Englishman, can like every American he ever met, and still dislike "Americans." It is a matter of the collective imagination. We have to break that image, replace it; there is no other way to redirect all that intellectual and moral energy away from its present Laocoön-like self-strangulation, into more fruitful forms of action.

But first we should take account of how much would be implied in accepting Graham Greene's version of the relations between the two cultures, and the historical pattern which that fits us into. The problem is not, has not been in the past, merely theoretical, or restricted to cultural matters. French distrust and resentment of England was an important factor in practical European politics of the nineteenth century; nowadays British dislike of America can be seen taking effect in every parliamentary debate on nuclear research, defense policy, or relations with Russia. To accept that dislike as inevitable and immutable is to accept a long future of halfhearted, bickering non-co-operation. Even more it is to accept the long-term corrosive effects of this "maturity" on ourselves internally. Again we can appeal to the historical pattern. Consider the political history of France since Waterloo; or of Italy in the sixteenth or seventeenth centuries; or of Greece under Rome. There were some great artistic and intellectual achievements, but as political organisms those countries were feeble, rancorous, and self-destructive. They somehow lost their self-respect along with their self-confidence when they began to think of themselves as more cultured, more mature, than their successful rivals. This is the really frightening possibility to me as an Englishman, implicit in the historical parallel, and in that part of our own thinking which justifies the parallel. Is that what England has in front of her, fifteen years of the Bourbons, eighteen years of the July Monarchy, the Second Republic, the Second Empire, the Third Republic, and so on, with scandals becoming more frequent, governments more precarious, and intelligent people more disaffected and cynical? Is there no way of avoiding that destiny?

Certainly we cannot deny its possibility, even probability. There is plenty of evidence in our recent development that we are headed in just that direction. Most of the changes that have come over England in the last twenty years—since the outbreak of the war—have been in that direction: she has been growing more like nineteenth-century France. England is becoming, that is, more interested in the arts and artiness, less serious about political and social action, more ready to find the truth bitter and complicated and impracticable, less willing to work for a cause, more completely reliant on personal advancement and appetite as the only effective motivations. The cheerfully pragmatic, eagerly active, simple and idealistic Englishman (the one Conrad was so taken with) is hard to find now.

Take, for instance, the Mediterraneanism now almost universal—even the farm laborers go to Paris in the spring. Angus Wilson pointed out in a recent story that every Englishman nowadays would prefer, if he could, to live outside England; and it is most typically to the Mediterranean countries he wants to go, or somewhere equally sunbathy, pagan, and arty. People have always complained of British weather, of course, and rich people have long gone to the Riviera; but the vast majority of the population have always, up to now, instinctively felt such places to be flimsy, unreal, rather ridiculous—England was after all the real workaday place, where the world's pulse beat. Now England is neither an important work place nor a good play place; it's merely drab; the truth is the English just don't know how to live! Now the Latin races know how to enjoy themselves! This mood is introducing incongruous Left Bank touches into the stolidity of Huddersfield and Sheffield and Chester. Everywhere now you find those dim-lit, often underground, *espresso* bars, called "Caprice" and "Macabre," where you see young men and women, half of whom work in a solicitor's office and live in a red-brick semidetached, wearing gamboge and green and discussing Cocteau. Before the war the few such people there were had no public meeting places in provincial cities. Now you see the sixth-form boys from the grammar schools sitting beside them and among them, accepting artiness and Mediterraneanism as a part of intellectual growing up.

Then the political life of the country is losing out in excitement and vigor to the arts. In a recent series of articles for the Manchester *Guardian* Anthony Howard has pointed out how feeble and unsuccessful the Labour party's youth organizations are, and how largely nonpolitical the Conservatives'; the one successful serious political organization for young people is "The Universities and Left Review Club," and there the politics is largely nonparty, extraparty, or postparty. The recent spurt of interest in the Liberals, which quite openly derived from boredom with the two major parties, has already died away. The big issues, like the nationalization of steel, seem quite unreal; foreign policy, when any initiative is taken, has an air of fantasy—the Suez adventure reminds one fatally of Napoleon III's military escapades. (Mr. Macmillan, though so much more intelligent, reminds one of that Emperor in the way his personality refers one so steadily back to a more glamorous past, in his case one of Etonian, Edwardian splendor.) Within the parties themselves politics has become nine-tenths machinery. Discipline is so rigorous that, despite the complete reversal of policy over Cyprus (up to a few weeks before the settlement it was declared that no British government, even Socialist, could possibly grant the island autonomy), despite this, no explanation of the change was thought necessary by the chiefs to the party members or by the party to the country. In natural consequence, as many writers have recently commented, the quality of M.P.'s is declining. Two of the very few Conservative members who dared criticize the Suez expedition when it began have been repudiated now, two years later, by the Conservative associations in their constituencies. They will not be sponsored for re-election. With this background, it is easy to understand why so much quasi-political excitement is aroused by, for instance, John Osborne; by the Angry Young Men in general; by that scuffle between two groups of them at a theater last year. All this seems more real, more truly political, than what the parties are doing. What it reminds one of, too often, is the literary-political battles of the 1830's in France, and the contempt for bourgeois parliamentary politics that went with them.

133

Lastly, of this obviously random sampling, take the young Englishman now to be found in such numbers in America; in all the Eastern colleges, in the English departments of every fair-sized university, in publishing, editing, advertising in New York, in every kind of cultural job, you find some of the brightest young Englishmen of their generation, in voluntary exile. Those who came over first on Fulbrights will be from the top third of their year at Oxford and Cambridge, and as a whole they will represent the most energetic and enterprising part of their country. Inevitably they are also the most corrupt. They come here partly because life is easier here, but also because the pulse of life is stronger; they suffer less from certain kinds of mutilation by coming than by staying; but inevitably they do suffer. They can't take root here; to do that an immigrant must start from the bottom. These young men start from the top. They are welcomed as finished products, cut blooms, *objets d'art*. Their reason for being welcomed is their unordinariness. It's a small step from that to feeling an adventurer, and an imposter. This feeling is discernibly a part of the atmosphere when such young Englishmen meet, nowadays, even before they come to this country. This kind of exile now suggests itself to intelligent young men at Oxford and Cambridge.

Not to mention, of course, the established British entertainers and performers who are settled over here more or less permanently. What are the qualities that add up to Britishness in Beatrice Lillie, Hermione Gingold, Cyril Ritchard, Noel Coward? Audacity, irony, edge, bite, polish—it's not what we used to mean by "so British."

All these, and many other, changes are in the direction Liebling indicated, away from bluff, hearty, kindly John Bull, toward the subtle Greek, the wily Florentine, the cynical Frenchman. It is our turn, in the historical pageant, to take on the psychology of "maturity," to behave and feel like the onlooker who sees most of the game. We must accept it; at least we must accept the loss of our old size, along with our old innocence; that superior height and weight, that psychological-moral solidity, that "any Englishman can beat ten Frenchmen in any fair fight." We are condemned to nervousness, self-consciousness, irony, prudence. But we are not condemned to an Old Etonian Second Empire, or red-brick Machiavellianism. Or to "Let's pretend it's Capri" in Hyde Park. Or to the spitefulness about America of the poem we began with. Irony and prudence can still be honorable. Our consciousness of the difference between our present state and our past, between ours and the American role in world affairs, can still be translated into an image which preserves our self-respect, which harmonizes and harnesses our energies.

For an image does not reflect the facts of a situation so much as the meaning of those facts for the mind that scrutinizes them. It reflects the expectations, energies, generosities of that mind as well as the statistical and historical material it is working on. So that Robert Graves's and Graham Greene's image of England-and-America may be true for them without being so for us, if the general temper of our minds is different; that image is only one of the possible interpretations of the situation. It has the support of many facts; insofar as it is generally accepted it is now creating more such facts in its own support—their readers *do* dislike and resent America after reading their books; but there are other facts, about the two countries' roles toward each other in the modern world, which would support a quite different image. There are other possibilities, as an image, some of which would lift England out of Liebling's historical pattern, and all its implications for our future; which would, if generally accepted, create facts of our behavior in its own support; which would give us back our self-respect. And only we, the British, can find such an image; that responsibility is in itself the definition of our role and the beginning of our self-respect.

The current double image is found on both sides of the Atlantic, of course; most Americans accept the "innocence" idea, most Englishmen are ready to think of themselves as ancient Greeks. But the responsibility for changing it lies more with us. The inferior in any situation is always more constantly and acutely aware of its implications. The superior can be slow-witted and generous, and can half-forget his superiority half the time. In the nineteenth century, though the English had, of course, images of the French and the Russians, these were on the whole crude caricatures, which intelligent people rose above; intelligent Britishers were aware how many foreigners were just as brave as, and far more intelligent than, the average Englishman. But even first-rate French and Russian minds had this vivid image of the Englishman—and they convinced even us of its truth. They were the image-makers of their day. So it is now; America will believe more or less what we tell her of our mutual dislike; but having believed it, she will act on that assumption, and both countries will find themselves more and more resembling their stereotypes.

2. *Britain's General Picture of Herself*

All that has so far emerged about Britain's present state has derived from her image of America; the implications of this found widespread corroboration, but their source remained special. Historically the attitude the older country has taken to its more successful and vigorous rival has always been its most important single foreign relationship, but still that can only be a function of something else. To readjust that image, to find a better way to conceive of that relationship, we must first get some idea of Britain's general relation to herself, general picture of herself, which necessarily controls the other, by its pervasive self-confidence or self-disparagement, by its power and truth or its halfheartedness, by its general convincingness. It is because, for instance, Englishmen think or suspect that their country is "in decline" that they resent America's growth; if they could really believe she was entering a new phase of development, might achieve a new kind of greatness, they could feel differently about the U.S.A. It is because they think of themselves as "gentlemen" who aren't quite gentlemen that they resent Americans' spontaneity and self-confidence; if they could find something else they really are, and really want to be it, that resentment too would disappear. What, then, is Britain's general picture of herself now, and how adequate is it? What international role does she cast herself in for the future, and can she fulfill it?

Each group has its own picture, naturally, but the one most generally palpable and effective is the Conservative party's; the idea of the quaint, old-fashioned country, full of eccentrics and courtly characters, retaining its "greatness" in the eyes of the world, thanks both to surprisingly shrewd (beneath their Old World charm) statesmen, and to the initiative of "brilliant" adventurers. A countryside of thatched cottages clustering round Tudor or Georgian manors, but streaked across by Jaguars and jets; up to the minute as well as charmingly in the past. This has inspired some historical parallels—the New Elizabethan Age, which we can leave to Sir Philip Gibbs and the women's magazines, and more recently, comparisons of Mr. Macmillan and the Queen to Disraeli and Victoria. But its real aspiration is to make the present recall that decade or two before 1914, when England, already past her fiercest intensity of self-development, already half in the past, was above all conscious of her own greatness, relaxing and luxuriating in it, admiring herself for her own history, her wealth, all her idiosyncrasies, good and bad. This is the age that produced Mr. Churchill. This is the one living tradition in the British mind. To recapture something of that mood, and the power that went with it, is the nostalgia that gives the Conservatives a semblance of political meaning; to change that was what gave Labour its zeal.

The extraordinary thing was the way in which everyone took it for granted that this oozing, bulging wealth of the English upper and upper-middle classes would last for ever, and was part of the order of things [says Orwell]. After 1918 it was never quite the same again. Snobbishness and expensive habits came back, certainly, but they were self-conscious and on the defensive.

The Conservative party, then, wants to make Britain "great" again, in that sense, and the poignancy of its yearning derives from its acute awareness that she is no longer "great," nationally or internationally. It wants to preserve all the insignia and privileges of power after their natural life has ended, and to keep rejuvenating them against nature by adventurers' tactics like the Suez affair. The disastrous parallel of the French Second Empire jumps to the mind again, but our own recent history is full of more incisive proofs of the suicidal folly of any policy in which this is a factor.

A particularly vivid example, both of this kind of romanticism and of its consequences, is the career of T. E. Lawrence, Lawrence of Arabia. This is especially appropriate, because it comes from that pre-1914 period we are now imitating with much diminished vitality; if it was unrealistic then, it is much more so now.

As a boy and young man, with that combination of talents and psychological problems which makes an aspirant to heroism, Lawrence modeled himself, consciously or not, on the kind of hero we meet in John Buchan's novels. He devised for himself, that is, romantic costumes and titles; he trained himself in secret, in resistance to pain, and in dangerous adventure; he learned obscure Arabic dialects; add to this his sexlessness, his secret melancholy, his devotion to classical literature, his love of practical jokes, and you have the Buchan hero complete. John Buchan, of course, had taken over the figure from Kipling, only smoothing out the roughness and truthfulness, so that it was a romantic and nostalgic bromide, a boys' magazine version of the empire-maker, even before Lawrence adopted it. He modeled himself on a figure who quite clearly belonged to the past, to "more dashing times," to "England's great days"; he was in his own eyes "an Elizabethan in modern dress." But the conditions of war in the Middle East gave him a chance to bring to life this figure of which the American equivalent would perhaps be the Gary Cooper cowboy; and though he seems to have failed in particular missions as often as he succeeded, and certainly he never did anything very important, it was so clear to his superiors just what kind of brilliant adventurer he was being—a kind of modern Sir Walter Raleigh—that they accepted his work at his own valuation. They too yearned back to the great days. He had, also, great skill in getting his exploits talked about and exaggerated.

However, he would have remained only a minor figure but for a kind of propaganda he would never have used himself, but which he was able to get without taking responsibility for it, from an American. When America entered the war, Lowell Thomas was sent to Europe to create some pro-Allied propaganda, and then got himself attached to the Middle East Command. Lawrence, the Prince of Mecca, with his Bedouin bodyguard, his Arabic costumes, his secret missions, his Aristophanes in the original—Lawrence was perfect propaganda material. Thomas made a series of lectures and film strips about him, and when he showed them at Madison Square Garden immediately after the war, he was asked to bring them to Britain. As he had a year's tour of America arranged, he said he would not unless he got a personal invitation from the King, and Covent Garden to show them in. He got them both; the Establishment wanted a hero of the right kind, a picturesque figure for the people; the lecture ran six months in London, after the first brilliant first-night audience since before the war. Though Lawrence asserted, quite mendaciously, that he had not co-operated with this vulgar publicity (it was very Cecil B. De Mille stuff), it was this that made him the only war hero to capture the imagination of the whole nation, from top to bottom.

This was a very Conservative arrangement; the retiring, well-bred, typically upper-class hero had to be made personally appealing to the mob, the new democracy; so they got an American to do quite vulgar and unscrupulous publicity and then repudiated it. For this Conservative image of England, with its reaction against contemporaneity and democracy, necessarily inspires anti-Americanism. Lawrence was immediately taken up by Mr. Churchill, among many men of power, all of whom recognized in him the traits of a twentieth-century Raleigh. And when trouble broke out again in the Middle East, Mr. Churchill got Lawrence included—gave him full authority, according to Lawrence—in the British delegation to the Cairo Conference of 1921, where the frontiers of the area were drawn. His advice, at least, was partly responsible for the establishment of the Hashimite kingdoms, the alienation of Ibn-Saud, the violation of all national and democratic feelings. This was to be expected, since Lawrence saw statecraft in terms of brilliant personalities, dashing adventures, and national "greatness"; and Mr. Churchill did not distrust such a view. In other words, our whole disastrous policy in the Middle East can be directly traced to the power over the imaginations of those in authority of this essentially romantic and unrealistic image. That is the kind of brilliant young adventurer the Conservatives are still hoping for and encouraging young men to become; to whom they are ready to commit our destinies. A few men like that abroad, and few statesmen like Mr. Macmillan at home, and Britain, it is hoped, can continue her pseudo-Edwardian imposture indefinitely.

But if the Conservative party's picture of England is dangerous and discredited—unacceptable to anyone at all clear-sighted —the Labour Party just hasn't one. Its reason for being was to redress the injustices and inequalities that were so crude and complacent before 1914. It did that in its 1945-52 period of office, and now it has nowhere to go, nothing to do.

The picture that most appeals to Labour voters, probably, is that of the neat, clean, classless little democracy, a bigger Sweden or Switzerland, with everybody busy and cheerful, and no Minister for Foreign Affairs. The countryside here would of course be urban, and very much of this century, with all the best features of the new towns. This is a good deal more honorable than the Conservative myth, but no more realistic; there are three cardinal features of our situation it leaves out of account; our language, which puts us in a special relation to America; the Anglo-Saxon culture we are responsible for to the world; and the Commonwealth. Any one of these would be enough, by itself, to prevent England's finding her true destiny in any conception of herself as a small, second-rate, self-contained power. Each one of them loads her with world responsibilities and promises, with possibilities of one or other kind of greatness, of first-rate power. If, endowed with those responsibilities and those promises, she assimilated herself to the Scandinavian or Benelux countries, out of the main current of events, she would neither have enthusiasm for what she was doing nor believe in it. There is, moreover, a Socialist inspiration in this picture which carries with it another kind of antagonism to America. The ideal citizens of this England would find Americans as egotistic, philistine, and vulgar as do the Conservatives' gentlemen, and so entangle themselves in the same self-destructive resentment. This idea of the country's future is as dangerous, in its opposite way, as the other.

Of the other general ideas, less connected with politics, the most powerful is that created by the writers and teachers of the country; the England of the universities and public schools, of London squares and literary cocktail parties, of long walks and village inns; and that is as reactionary, in another way, as the Conservative party's. Intellectual and artistic life since 1900, down to the morality of the sermons and the teaching of history in the schools, has suffered as much as politics and statecraft from arrested development, romanticism, unreality. There has been no imaginative assimilation of either the industrial or the scientific revolutions, which is to say, the whole corpus of modern life; in fact, cultural England today is *more* ignorant, uncomprehending, and hostile to all those facts than was the England of fifty years ago. The Victorian idea exhausted itself in the generation that was growing old in 1914, and the war, with all its destructiveness and all its challenges, made the break unusually final and complete. The exploration of the next phase of British life had already been begun, by D. H. Lawrence and E. M. Forster, but the courage to follow up that clue was destroyed by the war. The twenties preferred the ironic perpetuation and elaboration of social forms, of an idea of England, the artificiality of which they fully recognized. Vitality and seriousness were at a discount; the old images were cherished, precisely as old, in education and religion as in politics. Britain became an Old World country, specializing in traditions, class distinctions, and gentlemanliness. Boys were told to model themselves on Lawrence of Arabia and Rupert Brooke— working-class boys from Liverpool and Hull.

The result of this kind of choice can be seen in microcosmic form in quite a poignant recent essay by A. L. Rowse, Fellow of All Souls' College, Oxford, official historian of the Churchills, etc. Himself born of working-class parents, he says he responded during his youth very intensely and personally to D. H. Lawrence as the only writer who articulated much of his experience and awareness—"I was an unknown, unacknowledged younger brother." But Rowse went another way—*the* other way for a bright, sensitive boy of that class—up by scholarship into the Establishment. Lawrence, he decided, was *too* sensitive, too uncompromising, too rebellious; he destroyed himself. Rowse accepted the England he found, in all its artificiality and archaism; he assimilated himself to it, not vice versa. The poignancy lies in what he reveals without realizing, for he still thinks he was right. But a passage like this tells its own story:

It is the end of a civilization. Piper and Betjeman, Osbert Lancaster, Gerald Berners, Martyn Skinner, Jack Simmons, all my friends are right. In the heroic days of 1940-45 I used to put up a resistance and argue that there was a future. Now I know that they are right. There is no point in resisting any longer. It is the decay of a civilization that I study—like Leland and Aubrey before me; the one 'roving maggoty-headed' about the country wishing that there were monasteries still for such as he to retire into; the other ending up off his head, the spectacle of dissolution and destruction too much for him. Yes, it is a vanishing culture that I pursue, the debris that I lovingly cherish.

The same mood can be found in Betjeman's poetry, the collected edition of which has just sold forty thousand copies—the greatest popular success of the century for poetry in England.

Their civilization, their England, is indeed finished; but it was always a factitious thing, and we need mourn only for those thousands of the most intelligent of the last two generations whose lives were impoverished by their attempt to adapt themselves to it. For their civilization was an attempt to prolong pre-1914; it was a set of habits, and a set of values, in educational and artistic matters, strictly parallel to the political romanticism of T. E. Lawrence. Modern British conditions of life—leveled-down incomes at home, fewer colonial jobs abroad, no place for "brilliance" in either—demanded a different type from what the schools were producing, the professions demanding, the whole Establishment encouraging. The public schools were still producing men of action of the kind celebrated by John Buchan, men of sensibility like those in Norman Douglas. And after 1911 the new state secondary schools started making paler reproductions of these types. And what did they find to do in the world? Anthony Powell's and Angus Wilson's novels give a comic answer, Graham Greene's and C. P. Snow's a more serious one; all agree they found life mostly a matter of limitations, frustrations, unpleasant surprises. It was not what they had been led to expect. The world had no place for them, their talents and virtues any more than their weaknesses. They were pre-1914 types, molded in the images of those times, set loose in a post-1914 world. They never understood or accepted the existence of factories, mass production, advertising, the radio, television, universal literacy, atomic physics, economics, or psychiatry. Inevitably, they, more than anyone, found America and its inhabitants absurd, distasteful, alarming. They, and their England, felt themselves to be living in the wrong century.

This myth of England as much as the other two, then, lacks all real energy, conviction, appeal, and leads inevitably to that fatal resentment of our more vigorous rival which we began with. We must start again from scratch. We must remind ourselves of those other features of England's heritage and situation which can characterize her as a whole in quite another way, and can offer her a quite different relationship to the younger power. In her heritage we can recall its last great nineteenth-century manifestation, and the nongentlemanly, non-Old World forces that were dominant then; the great traditions of moral earnestness, of middle-class forthrightness, skepticism, and practicality. In her present situation, there are the three cardinal features mentioned before, the Commonwealth, the common language, the cultural responsibility.

The existence of the Commonwealth means that Britain is destined to political and international greatness again. The resources of Canada, Australia, the Union of South Africa, India, Pakistan, the new African territories, all united, in spite of so much, and after so long, by so strong a centripetal impulse; all this constitutes a potentiality far greater than Russia's or the U.S.A.'s. But as soon as one compares it with China, a necessary qualification becomes clear; China's greatness lies in the immediate future; one can measure its approach and the form it will take. The Commonwealth develops imperceptibly, if at all. This is not primarily a matter of population statistics, but it is significant that Australia only this year reached ten million inhabitants. It is calculated that it could support at least sixty million without any lowering of the standard of living, and the country has been in process of population now for nearly 150 years. The conditions of life are perfectly good. It is the *idea* of Australia that is dim—that is merely a larger, looser, diluted England. Why is Nehru unique among Commonwealth Prime Ministers in being a recognizable voice in international affairs? Why is Canada so immeasurably less important than the U.S.A.? Than France? Than Egypt? The answer to these questions must include her immaturity, her lack of self-responsibility, her status as daughter nation. The Commonwealth family of nations works well because there is no equality of energy or experience among its members; there is one adult and the others all acknowledge her authority. The centripetality is mostly lack of centrifugality —inertia.

In other words, we don't know what the Commonwealth will be when the member nations come of age; we only know they one day will. So though Britain cannot accept herself as a second Sweden, must continue to be a world power of some kind, she cannot find out from the Commonwealth just what kind. She cannot think of herself now as "the leader of the Commonwealth family of nations," with all the political and international power that implies. Toward the dominions she has only the simple duty to arouse them to self-responsibility, self-awareness, identity. She must continue to guide her own development as if she were responsible primarily to herself—to England, the great cultural entity.

Ultimately, of course, she is responsible for that development to the whole world. This is the second thing that distinguishes her from Switzerland. Anglo-Saxon culture is the dominant force in the Western mind, and the Western mind dominates the world. Communism's appeal to the uncommitted is significantly negative, as the *non*colonial power, the friend *against* those in authority. And for historical reasons Britain will always be the senior guide and guardian of that culture. The youngest American poet is likely to learn from Wordsworth; and one understands Wordsworth best, feels him most, in his own place and time. This is perhaps Britain's primary task in the modern world, finding her role in the Anglo-Saxon cultural partnership, reinterpreting, recreating, creating in its modern meaning for the rest of the world, the Anglo-Saxon mind.

Within the Anglo-Saxon partnership, America will surely have the more bountiful and multifarious vitality, will theorize, experiment, rebel, leap higher, fall lower. She is likely to have the greater power of originality and spontaneity; we must expect to be ironical and prudent, reflective and critical. It would be Britain's share, perhaps, to submit theory to tests of tough practicality, to relate sensation to integral moral experience, to ask always, "Is this honorably livable?" But to perform this task, play this role, she would need, of course, a different idea of herself as a culture, and that culture's typical human product, from that of the last fifty years. What is needed is a modern British type which has some vigor and glamour, and which is adapted to modern conditions, which has no desire for elegance or panache, no nostalgia for past greatness, which can accept poverty and irony without losing zest for life, which will feel itself at home in an overpopulated, postindustrial, postimperial, rainy little island in the North Sea; and I believe, of course, that she could find such a type in the decent man described in the last essay. The working of the cultural partnership with the U.S.A., moreover, becomes easy to imagine, once we learn to see Britain in that image, because of the peculiar authority the British middle-brow author has always had for the American reader. Lawrence, Leavis, Orwell, and Amis are most directly and practically concerned with the present, not in the least nostalgic for a plutocratic past; and these authors are exactly the people to test theory out in terms of practical effect, to consider everything as moral experience, to ask, "Is this honorably livable?"

The last feature of Britain's situation which made it seem impossible to plan a future for her like Sweden's or Switzerland's was the fact that she speaks the same language as America. It is often said that the likeness in speech conceals the great differences in thought, but I suspect that differences in language conceal the other kind even better; that if West Germany started speaking English as a native tongue tomorrow, America would soon discover far more profound differences from her than from Britain. What is written in England is read in America, and vice versa, far more quickly and widely than happens with any other two countries; and the inevitable consequence of that is that they think alike. Above all, this immediate awareness of the other's feelings—like a blood relationship—this use of an identical vocabulary, makes Britain the natural interpreter of America to the world, and of the world to America. Every time an Englishman opens his mouth the world acknowledges that here is someone close to the sources of power, a first-class, not a second-class, citizen of the world.

Of course this has its disadvantages. One of the characteristically ironic and corrosive joys of being born in England in this century is that one can earn a living anywhere in the world merely by teaching people to speak the language he has as a birthright—a silver spoon that was in his mouth when he was born—which is yet not *his* birthright. He is Jacob pretending to be Esau. It's American English the Turk and the Dane want, but they would rather learn the language from an Oxonian than from an American because his accent is so much better. This is the apotheosis of shabby gentility—the impoverished older branch living off its relationship to the reigning house and sneering at their vulgarity as they do so. But this irony is only corrosive because of the general context of resentment, mockery, and humiliation in which it occurs. If we can find a way of thinking, above all of feeling, about the two countries which alters that general context, which leaves both their self-respect, the community of language will give Britain a world function that will only reconfirm her pride. In any case it means that Britain's relation to America is of primary importance, whether for good or for evil.

None of the three current ideas of Britain's international role is vital or valid enough, then, to save her from rancor and pettiness. Nor does her position within the Commonwealth help us to form an immediate image of her beyond the fact that she cannot accept secondariness. But in examining these ideas we have discovered both how much Britain needs to change her general picture of herself and how essential to her is the link with America. Even, rudimentarily, we have discovered what that change and that link must involve. What we need now is to translate our findings into mythical form.

3. An Offering of Symbols

First of all, as a general historical picture of herself now, Britain has as much right to compare herself to the Athens of the fourth century B.C. as to Athens under Rome; and there is far more power for life in the earlier comparison. I mean the period after the death of Pericles, and after the crumbling away of the military and commercial empire he had established. Athens had become again only one of the ever-quarreling Greek cities; militarily, the future lay with the much younger, only partly Greek, Macedon; culturally, it lay with the very different kind of Hellenism which was spread over the world by Alexander's enormous conquests. And yet this was one of the greatest periods in Athenian history, with a kind of greatness available and desirable to England now. This was not most importantly or characteristically a matter of artistic achievement. It was a mode of interaction of philosophy and politics, of intercourse between action and speculation, made honorable and fruitful by pride in a great living past, and by (critical) faith in great democratic institutions. It was natural to a period of reflection after exhausting efforts, both successes and failures, when crude vitality was lower, but when just for that reason the intelligence and the conscience could make their voices generally heard. In Demosthenes you had one of the finest marriages of the practical with the idealistic in politics; in Socrates and Diogenes, the most fruitful kind of austerity and skepticism, of disciplined reaction against "greatness." In Aristotle's tutoring of Alexander, and Plato's experience at the court of Syracuse, you see the immediate availability to practical uses characteristic of that Athenian wisdom even at its most academic.

England is in many ways at a similar point in its historical development now. Athens's distinguishing feature was its homogeneity, the way all these brilliant men knew every side of each other so well, as complete personalities, not as a style in painting or a trend in philosophy; and judged such aspect as part of a complete life-in-society. This gave Athenian wisdom a uniquely practical, civilized, humanized character—every part of it was directly related to "how to live." And this homogeneity is a feature of British society today, despite the size of the population. Modern communications make every civilized country as homogeneous as a much smaller one in the past, and in England the taxes, the death duties, all the machinery of the Welfare State, and most especially the tremendously sifting and concentrating system of education, make it possible for one educated Englishman to know all about another in fifteen minutes' conversation. Every feature of British culture is in vivid and measurable relation to every other feature; whether you drink tea or coffee at breakfast, whether you pour the milk into your cup before the tea or vice versa, everything places you. The signs and symptoms are much more simply and universally valid there than they are in a multifarious country like the U.S.A. Add to this the awareness of a great living past, great institutions, and a great culture, along with all the disaffectedness and disingenuousness of the glory-gone, youth-past, popular mood, and you have some striking similarities of situation. Where are our Socrates and Diogenes? Read *Homage to Catalonia* and *The Common Pursuit;* read Orwell's *England, Your England,* and D. H. Lawrence's *England, My England.* There is *our* nose for the truth, the sour healing truth about us, our sharp self-questioning sanativeness, our unrelenting asperity. Once we recognize these books and these men as the significant ones of our time, once we see Britain mirrored in them more truly than anywhere else, we shall know how to build outward from that an image of a whole civilization, democratic, discursive, humanist, practical. A civilization concerned with the present not the past, with moral not aesthetic criteria, with honorable living not picturesque killing or being killed.

The typical British countryside of this image of Britain would be neither the Old World rurality of the Conservative and cultural picture, nor the Utopian Garden city of the Labour idea, but that mixture of nineteenth-century industrial devastation and twentieth-century council-house rehabilitation amid which most Englishmen do actually live. The Midland wilderness of slate roofs and smokestacks round Birmingham and Wolverhampton, or Northern towns like Wigan or Sheffield, could come to seem the natural setting for truth-telling of Orwell's kind, as much as olive trees and temples and blue skies do for Socrates. And if the Anglo-Saxon culture carried over the world by America is not dominantly, or even characteristically, British, we, as much as Athens in her day, can be responsible for the best of it.

The civilization I foresee would be one in which the past would be primarily the great Victorian period, history the understanding of how we developed from that to the present, and the future primarily a co-operation with America; in which education would prepare the cleverest boys and girls to live in and love present-day conditions and opportunities, present-day normality and decency; in which culture would make itself available uncondescendingly to the mass of the citizens. It would be a democracy, socially and culturally as well as politically and economically; still a great power, with great international responsibilities, but these for the time being mostly advisory and avuncular; for the Commonwealth it would be the tutor honestly eager to become merely the leader, for America the mediator between her and the rest of the world. Toward Americans its citizens would feel both a significant differentness and a significant similarity—a family likeness, in which one was allowed to be more spontaneous and the other more critical, but without mutual resentment.

For the political relationship between Britain and America there is no historical parallel with an implicit power for life. It seems as if no nation has ever yielded up leadership without an all-corrosive resentment of the younger country, and loss of faith in herself. But then no nation before has retained a position as a world power on other grounds—a position with a future—or has shared responsibility for a great culture so equally with the younger power, or has stood between her and the rest of the world by virtue of a common language and a common history.

America and Britain have the chance to create a kind of relationship between nations that would be new—the much older and retired brother's relation to the man in the bustling prime of life, with a family and dependents and a business and a hundred involvements. The relationship, let's say, of Sergey Ivanovitch to Kostya Levin at the end of *Anna Karenina,* or of Andrey Bolkonsky to Pierre Bezukhov in *War and Peace.* The older man is cooler, more skeptical, more cerebral, more detached; the other all boisterous exuberance, and then despondency. There are strains and tensions in such a relationship, in the novels and in real life; one would not hope to banish all distrust; but in the novels there is a more real trust and affection than there is yet between the two countries—in the novels there is an acceptance of each other. That is the key word.

If Britain would accept her present partial dependence on America generously and wholeheartedly, if she would identify herself—critically, of course—with America's interests, she could take a part in world affairs which would satisfy her. As leader of the Commonwealth, or as leader (a position which would not easily be granted her) of Europe, she would be a secondary power. With the one there is nothing to lead, the other refuses to be led by her—the Free Trade Area negotiations have shown how feeble are the sympathies, how easily aroused the irritations, between Britain and the Continent. But in relation to America, this elder brother's relation, she could be one of the four or five great nations of the world.

But only if she accepts that partial retirement and dependence. For some time, of course, she has had to admit America's greater power in international affairs. Just so she has long admitted the existence of American culture, by identifying that with bad films, cheap popular songs, horror comics. She has never yet accepted either fact. Recently, of course, since the London *Times* "Supplement on American Literature," there have been more serious discussions of American novels, though there are still only two or three men in all the British universities employed to teach American literature full time, and neither Oxford nor Cambridge offers any series of lectures on the subject. But most of this new interest is neither intelligent nor wholehearted. It either remains academic or concentrates on the exotic, and is likely to create an Americanization as false and superficial as the Europeanization Orwell used to complain of in British intellectuals. It delights in Raymond Chandler and juvenile delinquents and jazz slang and Southern Gothic. It still does not take America seriously as our successor, our collaborator, in reinterpreting, recreating, creating the Western mind.

The way to that acceptance is clear. Britain as the country of decency, middle-brow, puritan, lower middle class, could afford to acknowledge all America's more gaudy achievements as her contribution to the Anglo-Saxon partnership. Herself temporarily more limited, her powers in abeyance, though not in decline, her experience much more available as wisdom because of this temporary retirement, she would not feel a rival, or an inferior, or threatened. She would be able to accept, and benefit from, the extraordinary gush of American vitality, and she would find that she has as much to give in return. We could concentrate, purify, direct that gush away from the fantastic, the naïve, the vulgar, and help make it, in ourselves and in them, something honorable, practical, beautiful.

The images we started off with, the Englishman's idea of the American, and vice versa (Graves and his Superman and, in *The Quiet American,* Alden Pyle and Fowler), cannot be replaced by an act of will. So far these are the ways Anglo-Saxon writers have seen the two countries in confrontation. Perhaps they never will see this other truth. There is not even any contemporary *general* image of the American, or of the Englishman, to compare with those magnificent images of the nineteenth-century Russian that Tolstoy created in Kostya Levin and Pierre Bezukhov. But though very differently focused, very unintended for this function, the two national personalities I believe in are discernible in the novelist's persona characters in Kingsley Amis's novels and the central figures in J. D. Salinger.

Lucky Jim, with his healthy, open, ordinary face (a good example of the decent man I described at the end of the last essay), teacher of history at a provincial university, rebelling against all the artiness and Mediterraneanism of the Welches, all the archaism of Merrie England and madrigals and warming pans, trying to return to simple moral imperatives and healthy human contact and all-round decency. Zooey Glass, the Jewish-Irish TV actor and scholar in classical Greek, extravagant in his talents, his temperament, his moods and his manner, content with nothing less than perfection, contemptuous of and resentful of everyone and everything that fails of that, and yet in contact, in love with them at the same time.

They have quite a lot in common; their distrust of contemporary intellectual society, their acute self-dissatisfaction, their very moral sense of humor, the love of fantasy seen in their elaborate lying and their disguised voices at the telephone, most essentially their passionate, all-exclusive search for sincere meanings in themselves and in one or two others, without which they cannot begin to live. In all this, both dramatize the same predicament, that of the highly intelligent young Anglo-Saxon today; they were both born into the ruling class of the world, in external matters comparatively unlimited, unoppressed, weightless, but their consciences heavy with guilt, with the fear of complacency or complaisance, with the responsibility to invent a completely admirable life; they are facing the same problems (how much is worldly, professional success—or failure—worth?), discarding the same outworn solutions (complete idealism or complete cynicism), abiding by the same tests (of intelligence, of force, of decency, of manhood). The difference is that the American takes more risks, comes nearer to complete disaster, rises higher, ignores practical material difficulties more grandly. Zooey Glass gives himself an ulcer, and upsets his family, brooding over the problems of human nature and goodness and happiness, and seeks his solutions in the most difficult of religious philosophers. The Englishman is concerned to find a more humbly workable life, limits himself severely, does not attempt religion or philosophy. Lucky Jim's struggle with himself is not to marry the wrong girl out of pity, to find the courage to pursue the girl he wants, to keep his job without losing his self-respect. But they are the same sort. They would understand and like each other, if they knew each other. Above all, since each is an image of his country, in their conjunction we can see Britain and America facing and acknowledging each other without malice and without resentment.

I wasn't satisfied with that ending. I felt I hadn't made anyone see the genuine vision, sketchy and glimpsy though it was, that I had had; the confrontation of these two immensely likable, intensely representative young men; much less what that could mean in terms of national personality. One would have to go back to the creators themselves, and listen to the two proses; their similarity, for instance.

His mouth, which had all the mobility of a partly collapsed inner tube, was incompletely encircled by a brownish grime of stubble; his greying hair came horizontally out of his scalp and projected in two still inorganic shelves over his ears; his eyes, long and heavily lidded, glared a little. . . . Distinctly, her ways of holding it tended to blow to some sort of literary hell one's first, strong, (and still perfectly tenable) impression that an invisible Dubliner's shawl covered her shoulders. . . . Her utterance, than which none in the whole semantic field could have incited me to a more profound assent, was delivered in a whisper so close to my ear that I felt her warm breath. . . . A feat, I haven't a doubt, that will eventually win me the Eastern Philosophy Chair in Hell.

One and three are Amis, two and four Salinger, but the two sensibilities can hardly be distinguished.

You would have to go back and see Jim Dixon, with his "healthy," innocent, ordinary face, against the dual background of his Welsh university town, the two ways of life; on the one

155

side, the thousand upon thousand of bay-windowed, linoleumed little houses, set edge to edge up narrow hilly High Streets or —slightly larger houses—separated by private hedges along broad, quiet residential areas; and on the other side Professor Welch's house, full of French novels and chi-chi paintings and ballet dancers and Bohemians; and see him trying to find, by some combination of these possibilities, something to want and fight for, something to believe in and sacrifice for. And behind him you must set Orwell and Lawrence and Leavis and the composite figure I described at the end of "British Decency." (I had still not identified the source of that inspiration, the guiding idea I had followed.)

And opposite him put Zooey Glass, barking into the loud-speaker of his phonograph, lying on his back on the floor talking, set against the dual background of New York; on the one side, the vast, sordid, sinister jungle-city most clearly presented in The Catcher in the Rye, *where a laugh at midnight goes echoing down the street, and where the Fat Lady has the radio on all day; and on the other side the Antolinis' elegant apartment and the Wicker Bar, and the whole world of successful writers, directors, actors, publishers; and Zooey's identical struggle to put together, out of that mosaic of luxury and delinquency, of philistinism and creativity, a pattern that will satisfy his self-respect as well as his ambition. And behind him I can set the young writers and teachers in this country whose efforts so impressed me when I first came over in 1952.*

Both these figures suffer a strong temptation to retreat, the American to the religious life, monastic or private, the Englishman to the working classes; but these are consciously, admittedly, escapes; and duty, for both of them, remains in some sense avowedly the intellectual life, as teacher, librarian, actor, writer. And they guide themselves, in that life, by the same kind of values. One knows that Zooey Glass would feel the

156

same way as Jim Dixon about Professor Welch and his family, and Vernon Gruffydd Williams and his friends; one suspects that T. S. Eliot would not. One knows both Zooey and Jim would dislike Basil Seal and Sir Henry Harcourt-Reilly if they met them, and would be sure to vote the other way in elections.

The difference between them is that the American is much more a remarkable person, claiming a remarkable destiny as of right. His looks, his intelligence, his talents, his personal power, are all exceptional. The Englishman claims to be ordinary, to be decent, at best. But the crucial dividing line in the world, for both of them, is that between the phonies and the people they like and trust. They would draw that line in more or less the same place. They notice more or less the same gestures in any public figure presented to them, and they interpret those in more or less the same way. Both are in love with the present, with all its disadvantages, and not with any past.

"Mirror for Anglo-Saxons" did, as I had hoped, return my argument to its starting point, and brought out why it should be the experience of America that led me to question, criticize, and sift out my loyalties to England; but while I was writing it I realized that there was one more thing to be done. Those loyalties that did survive criticism, that gained immensely in vigor from it, must be put in another perspective, in their historical relation to the great English achievements of the past. I kept coming across figures and conjunctions and scenes of decision, in various autobiographies, of this and the last century, which clarified and dramatized for me the process by which England had acquired its present, false, official face; how and why the essential Englishness of Lawrence, Leavis, and Orwell had been so obscured that I had had to discover it for myself, how and why much less important and typical figures had been presented to me as essentially English, how and why cultural history had been falsified.

157

THE CULTURAL CRISIS:
A BACKGROUND

1. The Wrong Choice

Maynard said, "What is really important is that we can't go back on this. Whatever may develop neither side can start the war up again. The troops would not fight and the people would not work." This was a more common sense argument than Lawrence's and with it in my mind I went to bed and fell fast asleep.

It was Maynard Keynes, later patron of the arts and adviser to the government, who said this to David Garnett, later prize-winning novelist and essayist, and the occasion was very late at night on Armistice Day, 1918, when they were both brilliant young men. It was earlier in that same day that Garnett had met D. H. Lawrence, who had said,

This war isn't over. Even if the fighting should stop, the evil will be worse because the evil will be dammed up in men's hearts and will show itself in all sorts of ways which will be worse than war.

As is usual in such dramatic conflicts, both were right and both were wrong; they weren't talking about the same thing; but it was all the more significant a conflict for that—which things *should* one be talking about?—and Garnett's choice of which to listen to sprang from a thousand causes and carried a thousand

158

consequences. Should one think in terms of "the evil in men's hearts" or in terms of "guilty governments" and "innocent peoples"? Should one look forward eagerly to a future of the sophisticated, libertarian hedonism, to which Keynes's Bloomsbury friends were already calling the tune, or angrily to the rootless, jazzy, jagged dissipation Lawrence foresaw? These were to be, it turned out, the basic alternatives for the country, but David Garnett was perhaps the only man to have them presented to him so early, simply, dramatically, and straight from the horses' mouths. This was not exceptional for him; he was young, handsome, eager, everyone's favorite disciple; he had spent Armistice Day going from party to party, canvassing every reaction. Between these two episodes he had been dancing in the streets, with Lady Mond, wife of the great industrialist and financier, out in Trafalgar Square in the shifting crowds of excited, rejoicing Londoners. It was there he had made his decision. "The temper of the crowd was enchanting. Lawrence was wrong. All were sick to death of hatred and were purging it out of their hearts in an outburst of universal love." He made up his mind; the future was to be fresh and brilliant, free of all the faults of the past; he committed himself to the Keynesian interpretation.

Lawrence was the only person who talked in that strain at Garnett's parties that day; he had become a very isolated figure. It was even then some time since the two men had met, for Garnett had made the fundamental choice between Lawrence and Keynes—and the Stracheys and the Stephens, etc.—in 1915. Again the choice had been perfectly conscious and clear-cut. Lawrence had written him a letter warning him against the influence of some of his friends—Keynes, Frankie Birrell, Duncan Grant, the Stracheys. Lawrence had recently met some of these people during his visit to Cambridge; for in those days, when he thought of a joint lecture series to be given with Bertrand Russell, he was not essentially isolated. *Sons and Lovers* had had a great success, and through Middleton Murry and Katherine Mansfield, and Edward Garnett and Ottoline Morell,

Lawrence had got to know and like most of the young writers of the time; it was a time of youth and rebellion and gaiety and renewal, and Lawrence was perhaps the gayest and most youthful of all. But as his ideas developed they became more challenging—*The Rainbow* and *The Crown* were much less well liked than *Sons and Lovers*—and he himself began to realize that all these new friends were not moving in any parallel direction to him, that all these forms of gaiety and rebellion were not to his sense healthy. He expressed his feelings about these friends to Garnett by comparing them with beetles—the hard, shiny, brittle carapace, the squashiness, the aversion from sunlight, etc. They didn't seem to him naturally living, naturally growing things. Garnett had not needed to deliberate long before making up his mind. "Lawrence's letter made me angry. He seemed to me to be mad and determined to interfere in my life. I therefore decided not to see him again." And when they did meet again, that Armistice Day, for the last time, it was no real meeting. Garnett took his life direction from the other people, from Bloomsbury, instead; and this was a crucial choice, a symptomatic choice, of much more than personal significance, because it was motivated so purely and intelligently by the essential qualities of two kinds of men.

In his reminiscences of these events Lord Keynes makes light of any opposition Bloomsbury may have had to offer Lawrence —"poor silly clever us"—but that was not how it seemed at the time, to Garnett or to them. They were molders of men. In 1917 and 1918 Lytton Strachey visited the farm where Garnett, Duncan Grant, and Vanessa Bell were living at the time, and read out to them in the evenings *Eminent Victorians*, which he was then writing; and the listeners were conscious that the contemporary mood was being created in front of them, being given a form, a name, a myth. At one of his first meetings with Garnett, in 1914, Strachey had read out to a similar gathering a story of his, "somewhat in the manner of *Les Liaisons Dangereuses*," which had had the effect of reversing Garnett's sexual morality. He had been up to then "an unrepentant sentimentalist"; now "Lytton's little tract" made him realize that "sincerity was a chief virtue in love, or lust"; he realized that he was, by nature, a "libertine," a word which, with its synonyms, "rake," etc., mapped out a whole philosophy of love.

Obviously, here was a strong, intellectually formidable influence on his young friend directly inimical to all Lawrence believed. What is more difficult for us to realize is that in this tug of war Lawrence did not figure, at the time, as the newcomer or as the oddity. Garnett had gone on a walking tour in Germany with Lawrence and Frieda when they were first together, and before he knew the Stracheys and the Stephens. He had liked Lawrence very much, and had moreover recognized in him the essential Englishman, the working-class man, and the great lover, all of them very potent images, then, before 1914. Not to mention a genius. While he talked Garnett listened, admired, absorbed, worshiped, the perfect disciple. This was the time when Lawrence could seem a natural successor to Wells and Bennett, as representative of the emergent lower classes, and to Hardy and Meredith, as the celebrant of beauty and passion and freedom. Lytton Strachey was a much more bizarre and *outré* figure. He fitted into nothing. Except the future.

Lawrence too obviously represented a future, a development from the past that was a radical change. But Lawrence was recognizably—at that time—the next step in a progress Garnett's father, among many others of his time, had foreseen. They had foreseen more freedom in English life, more passion, more beauty, more gaiety, more sunlight; less convention, less morality, less Protestantism, less middle-classness. The country had been through its Roman period, in the nineteenth century, and now was going to be Greek. The pre-1914 novels of E. M. Forster and H. G. Wells are examples of this hopeful mood, and D. H. Lawrence could and did seem the Messiah of this expectation. And in such a theology Lytton Strachey could only appear as one of the feebler devils, with his sickliness, his Pyrrhonism, his formality of manner and irony of tone. It took the Great War to shatter that too innocent, too optimistic view of history, and give Strachey a new role as realist, clear-sighted moralist, and arbiter of manners.

But even before 1918 David Garnett had no difficulty in choosing between the two, when the necessity was made plain. And in him his whole generation may be seen choosing. For he was a perhaps uniquely representative figure. Born in 1892, the son of Edward and Constance Garnett, he inherited some of the best gifts of late Victorian radicalism. His father was the discoverer and encourager of Conrad, Lawrence, Hudson, and every kind of genius and talent. (He was the model for Bosinney in *The Man of Property*.) His mother was the translator of Tolstoy, Dostoevski, Chekhov, a Fabian, and a friend of Russian revolutionaries. They were both sturdy individualists, and their son was left free of all religious, social, or moral pressures. He was not sent to public school, or to Oxford or Cambridge; he traveled all over Europe, even Russia, alone, in his teens, and went to the Imperial College of Science in South Kensington, where Wells had been. He knew all the young writers, from Lawrence to Rupert Brooke. He moved among all the most advanced ideas and enthusiasms. And he responded to them; when he was seventeen he got involved in a plot to release some Indian prisoners of state in London, and risked some real danger. For—and this is his major claim to representativeness—he was a good-looking, warmhearted, lovable, natural, *normal* boy. This is attested by everyone—it was his role in Bloomsbury. They were all intelligent and talented; he alone was also simple, natural, happy. He was notorious for his good nature, for his happy love affairs, for his healthiness; he claims he was the only person in Bloomsbury, apart from Clive Bell, capable of killing cockroaches. The Stephens and the Stracheys were all predestined to eccentricity, of one kind or another, but David Garnett was unlimited, infinitely responsive, capable of every enthusiasm. He was enthusiastic about Lawrence, when he met him; he had a chance of accepting even that challenge: as much chance as anyone could have.

But after that Armistice Day in 1918, Garnett never saw

Lawrence again. His friends, his activities, his aspirations, his satisfactions all assumed un-Lawrentian forms. He and Frankie Birrell ran a bookshop, and lived pretty completely within the Bloomsbury world. He wrote *Lady into Fox,* won literary prizes, edited T. E. Lawrence's letters, is still writing novels about love and France and the art of living. From the point of view of immediate success he certainly made the right choice. T. S. Eliot presented him to France, in the *Nouvelle Revue Française,* as *"Il l'emporte sur tous les prosateurs contemporains pour l'habileté purement technique."* He spontaneously made the same general choices as his generation and they saluted a man of unusual taste and intelligence.

2. *The Last Generation*

David Garnett belonged to a generation; that is, a group of people of roughly the same age united by an identical mode of reaction against the past their fathers represented. Members of a generation feel that their fathers (and grandfathers, often —the whole immediate past) embodied an idea, or a set of ideas, that does not satisfy *them,* and they aspire toward a new idea of their own. Obviously, however small the nucleus of originators, their rebellion must win recognition and acknowledgment from more than a few of their contemporaries; obviously that recognition must be of hitherto unexpressed and powerful feelings in the auditors themselves. Every group of intelligent people whose ages range between twenty and thirty and who share the same interests feels itself to be in some sense a generation. But in the more important sense there has been only one generation in this century. That was the generation to which David Garnett belonged, of people born in the last twenty years of the nineteenth century, coming to maturity with the war.

This generation included D. H. Lawrence, Lytton Strachey, Virginia Woolf, etc., but it equally included Aldous Huxley, E. M. Forster, Evelyn Waugh, George Orwell, F. R. Leavis. They all found themselves living in their grandfathers' world, which their fathers had merely kept going. Its modes of being were all exhausted; they described them, according to their temperaments, as comic or tragic, they diagnosed or they denounced; they all rejected. George Orwell rebelled against Crossgates, Eton, and imperialism in Burma. F. R. Leavis rebelled against nineteenth-century academic taste and academic teaching. In the United States this was the generation of T. S. Eliot, Ezra Pound, John Crowe Ransom, Dos Passos, Hemingway; in Ireland of Joyce; in France of Proust. It was a time of major readjustment and renewal. The variety of solutions found to the common problem was almost infinite; but one can draw a broad distinction between two main kinds of rebellion in England. On the one hand, the Stephens and Stracheys (for example), who, though they started by rebelling against authority, succeeded so well that they themselves became authority. They became "the Establishment." On the other, Lawrence, Leavis, and Orwell (almost alone), who remained rebels all their lives, rebelling against their contemporaries when the ghost of their fathers was finally laid.

The Establishment is not, of course, to be equated with Bloomsbury; it was a hegemony in which Bloomsbury was merely one, though the central, party; but there was a minimum similarity of temperament and taste which united all the members of the hegemony, and marked off the outsiders; to define that common denominator we can go back for a moment to David Garnett. In his criticism of his father's generation we can detect the criterion that was to unite all the members of his own. Here is his description of Roger Fry and his own father, which is also of interest as illustrating the way members of a generation resemble each other and can be recognized.

Roger's hair, the line of his nose, jaw and neck, the roll of his eye and the cock of his eyebrow all reminded me of Edward and, perhaps because of this, I sometimes felt the impatience that a young man so often feels for his father. Roger also wore the kind of clothes which Edward had been accustomed to wear in middle life; a brown Jaeger shirt, a homespun loosely cut jacket and trousers which soon lost their shape, sometimes a tie of shantung silk. Both Roger and Edward had moreover much the same attitude to life. They were intolerant of the British public, the bourgeoisie, the villa residents, and of the British indifference to art. They both not only disliked the British way of life, with its shams, hypocrisy, respectability and censoriousness, but they denounced them in almost the same words, in tones of pitying exasperation. Both felt the same deep contempt for the British business man. Both had the same attitude to conventional morality.

One's first reading of this can leave one puzzled; did David Garnett, then, feel more kindly toward villa residents and the bourgeoisie, toward conventional morality and the British indifference to art? Obviously not. What he objected to was not the opinion, but the activism and expansiveness of it, the exasperation and denunciation and missionariness. He wanted something more sophisticated, more ironical and elegant, that would not take British conventions any more seriously, but would appreciate them, play with them, use them for its own ends.

And his friends quite independently felt the same way about their elders. Clive Bell's remarks on Roger Fry have the same tone; Roger was naïve, overenthusiastic, always slightly absurd. The Stephen children seem to have felt that about their father; too innocent, too clumsy, too patriarchal, too bearded. No adequate conception of the art of living; which for them meant perfect adaptation to one's social function; for them the center of the world was the personal relationship within the polite social complex, and work, causes, religion, abstract ideas were all to be subordinate to that. The Lehmann children, John, Rosamond, Beatrix, differed from their father in the same way. They made themselves smaller, lighter, more flexible figures. Weight, solemnity, ultimate responsibility were transferred out to institutions, traditions, etc., in compensation; in art and religion as much as in politics.

It is this taste for the elaborate, intellectually, aesthetically, even socially, which characterized the Establishment as a whole. A distaste for the simple, the morally intense, the categorical imperative; a need to work through forms and conventions and institutions, this is what unites such disparate figures as T. S. Eliot, Virginia Woolf, Evelyn Waugh, Graham Greene, etc. A correlative of this is the enthusiasm for all things French; France being seen as the country where the importance of forms was correctly understood. Clive Bell tells us that though Lytton Strachey struck his friends as uniquely the cultured man, this did not mean that he knew any more, or as much, of English literature as they, or of the classics; but he knew a lot about French literature. Of all periods it was the French eighteenth century that was most loved and celebrated. Geoffrey Scott's *Portrait of Zélide* is one example, and we have already come across Strachey's imitation of *Les Liaisons Dangereuses*. But one remembers T. S. Eliot's fascination with Laforgue and Corbière, with Baudelaire and Valéry. And the role of twentieth-century Paris in Elizabeth Bowen's novels and Nancy Mitford's. France in all periods is the touchstone of wit, irony, clarity, grace—civilization.

Lawrence, Leavis, and Orwell have never shared this enthusiasm. Orwell complained of the Europeanization of the English intelligentsia, Leavis has always held that the reputations of Flaubert and Proust in England are exaggerated, and the ideals of art these reputations reflect are inferior. And this is because none of the three has been in love with the elaborate and formal. Their truths have been intellectually simple and morally intense. What they rebelled against in the Edward Garnetts and the Roger Frys was not the missionary and clumsy fervor of the tone, but the irresponsible aestheticism of the message. Which was, of course, just what David Garnett and Clive Bell did accept.

And in this Lawrence, Leavis, and Orwell are the true, the legitimate heirs of the previous great generation, the previous great achievement in British life, Victorianism. They rebelled doctrinally, of course, even more than most of their generation, but the moral-temperamental heritage they accepted. They took life with the same intense moral seriousness. Lawrence celebrated passionate love as exclusively as George Eliot had celebrated compassionate love, but he did it with the same missionary spirit. (Compare Virginia Woolf.) Orwell disliked everything Carlyle stood for, but he disliked it with the same fervor. (Compare T. S. Eliot's social criticism.) Leavis's account of the great poets would be very different from Arnold's, but the intellectual, the emotional, and the moral are held in the same tension in the opinions of both men. (Compare anyone.) They remain recognizably the same kind of people as the authorities they attack. The Establishment did not rebel more radically, in matters of doctrine, perhaps less; and they managed to present themselves as typically, pietistically, English—the natural heirs of Carlyle, Arnold, George Eliot, etc.; but in point of fact they rejected the essential meaning the word "English" had had before their time.

It would be unfair to accuse the Establishment as a whole of sharing Lytton Strachey's opinion of the eminent Victorians, in any simple sense, but that book, that kind of silly, self-confident, self-mutilating rejection of the Victorian past, is one of the great documents of their rebellion, their new direction, their new mode of being.

3. Victorianism and Its Heirs

The Victorian Frame of Mind, by Professor Walter E. Houghton, is the most convincing exploration and definition I know of the attitudes and activities and assumptions of that generation. He limits Victorianism, in its essence, to the years 1830-70, and restricts his investigation to more or less typical intellectual attitudes. His central definition of the Victorian mind is that of a mind dominated by doubt, about the nature of man, society, and the universe, but a doubt coexistent with a wholehearted search for positive, final answers; the doubt remains in the modern world but our search for, our expectation of, positive final answers, is less wholehearted; so that the decisive contrast between the Victorian and the post-Victorian minds is that between Arnold and Pater—Pater standing for a kind of relativism, Arnold inflexibly against it. This relativism is ob-

167

viously not so much a matter of theory, of epistemology, as of practice; it is a diminution of the moral, the imperative element in the total response, the total judgment. Carlyle, Ruskin, Newman, Gladstone, Florence Nightingale, all in their different ways achieved an unself-conscious solemnity and intensity of assertion, a dramatic power and thrust of belief, that we identify as Victorian, and which Professor Houghton tells us was to be found in the quite minor prophets of the time, too, in the reviews and sermons and letters of thinking men.

By this definition it is easy to see that Leavis is the only Victorian among contemporary literary critics; in contrast with T. S. Eliot as well as with Lord David Cecil. And the puritanism Lawrence and Orwell are accused of is equally a matter of an unqualified hortatoriness, a disgust with the contemporary norm of polite velleity. Regardless of their general philosophical positions, they *felt* each opinion as absolutely true. They searched for positive answers in a wholehearted way.

Professor Houghton's chapter headings in his section "Intellectual Attitudes" sketch out the atmosphere Leavis creates around him today, today so sharply in contrast with everything else: "The Critical Spirit—and the Will to Believe," "Anti-Intellectualism," "Dogmatism," and "Rigidity"; the subheadings for that last chapter, "Sectarian Fervor," "Puritan Judgement," "The Need for Rigidity," and "The Open and Flexible Mind." The paradoxes there, especially in that last pair of phrases, are uniquely applicable, in the last generation, to the three men we are considering. What other critic than Leavis could speak of a need for rigidity, and *be* rigid, and at the same time remain supremely an open and flexible mind? Lawrence is surely our greatest puritan and dogmatist; and Orwell our best example of a union of the critical spirit with the will to believe; throughout his essays he diagnoses and dismisses political-cultural pretentions more bitterly and totally than anyone, and at the same time always emerges at the end with a minimum decent positive solution.

And consider this paragraph from the opening section of Professor Houghton's book:

Today we tend to think of the intellectuals as a special class, ahead of their time perhaps and certainly out of touch with professional and business life; and though exaggerated, the notion has its foundation in fact. But this divorce between the artist and the public—which can be seen on the Victorian horizon—did not occur until the last decades of the century. In the years between 1830 and 1870 the sense of crisis at the very moment when the traditional authority of the church and the aristocracy was breaking down, impelled men of letters to focus on the contemporary scene more consciously, I think, than they had ever done before; and then, in the light of their analysis, to urge the adoption of one or another political, religious, or moral philosophy. Moreover, at a time when middle-class achievements in commerce, industry, and politics were so extraordinary, the artist-thinkers were more imbued with bourgeois ideals and more sensitive to bourgeois needs than was later the case. On the other side, a large public living in an age of "doubts, disputes, distractions, fears" looked deliberately to the literary prophets, and to the famous reviews through which they usually spoke, for guidance or reassurance; and the captains of industry, so long as their formal education was so limited, turned to men of letters for the culture which a rising class is eager to acquire. No doubt certain attitudes—optimism, moral earnestness, and the worship of force, for example—were more common among the men of action, while others like melancholia and enthusiasm were more often found among the intellectuals. But all exist, in varying degrees, in both groups. The intimate connection between literature and life is a significant feature of the Victorian age and one of its chief glories.

That intimate connection Lawrence, Leavis, and Orwell, in their different ways, all labored to restore. That is the kind of artist-thinker Lawrence tried to be; that is the kind of review *Scrutiny* was intended to be; that is the function Orwell held up to contemporary intellectuals as their failed duty. They offered a substitute for the authority of the church and the aristocracy. They urged the adoption of political, religious, moral, or critical philosophies. Their *bête noire* has never been the bourgeoisie so much as the Sitwell class. They expected a large public to look up to them for guidance or reassurance. They were prophets. The one of their contemporaries who came nearest to taking on the same responsibilities is perhaps T. S. Eliot; and for him there is no intimate connection between literature and life, between the artist and the thinker; all the connections for him are elaborate, etiolated, institutional; there is no habitual, vital interchange. Whereas for the three puritans the Victorianism Professor Houghton describes is the true ideal of society to which they have tried to restore their contemporary England.

Lawrence, Leavis, and Orwell, then, are the true transmitters of the Victorian heritage. Their rebellion against Edward Garnett and Roger Fry could be described as a return to a purer form of that heritage. Whereas the Stracheys and Stephens reacted further away from it. For both Garnett and Fry belonged to a subgeneration, a partial revolt against Victorianism. They were born into peripheral groups (Garnett into the Pre-Raphaelite circle, Fry into the Quakers) and they were too young to have felt the full force of the idea in its 1830-70 period. They lived at a time when the Victorian impulse was failing and exhausted, when the peripheral groups had become more self-confident. They retained a certain moral size and energy in their personal relations and modes of expression, but in their thinking they had declined into a too simple excitement about freedom and beauty and art. If we compare them with Sir Leslie Stephen, the father of Virginia Woolf and Vanessa Bell, we see the difference; where they are enthusiastic for genius, passion, and beauty, he is for character, common sense, and moral goodness. Stephen belonged to the most central and vital tradition of the Victorian mind; he is one of the people Professor Houghton quotes and refers to most often.

Stephen's career, and his relation to Leavis, are an interesting paradigm of Victorianism and its transmission. In his autobiography, *Some Early Impressions,* he tells first of the evangelical Clapham sect family he was born into; doctrinally he rebelled against it, but the moral-temperamental heritage he acknowledged, accepted, developed throughout his life. The puritan, he says, "is a person for whom I have profound respect and much sympathy," and in fact, by modern standards, he was one himself. The next great influence upon him was Cambridge, where he spent fourteen years, and which he contrasts with Oxford as "for the last three centuries inclined to the less romantic side of things. It was for Puritans against the cavaliers, for Whigs against Jacobites, and down to my time was favoured by 'Evangelicals' and the good 'high and dry' school which shuddered at the development of the 'Oxford Movement.' " Where Oxford had Newman, Cambridge had the mathematician Todhunter, no spiritual leader but a good teacher whose personality was indistinguishable from the discipline of his subject; where Oxford had Jowett, he says, Cambridge had Whewell, massive of character, scornful of charm, son of a Lancashire tradesman. (Elsewhere Stephen speaks of "that shrewd, hard-headed, north-country type, which was so conspicuous at Cambridge.") In other words, he locates British academicism as we understand it today at Oxford, and sets the Cambridge of his time up in contradistinction to that. And endorses it.

He makes a convincing case for Cambridge then being a real intellectual community, but admits that there were no spiritual leaders in residence. Of the alternatives of that kind England was offering, Carlyle-Ruskin, Coleridge-F. D. Maurice, and John Stuart Mill, Cambridge and Stephen gave the bulk of their devotion to Mill. He seemed to them the strongest in common sense and realism, the freest from romanticism and obscurantism. Stephen and Cambridge prided themselves on their shrewdness, skepticism, and moral responsibility.

He left Cambridge, having ceased to be a Christian, and entered journalism in its golden age. He wrote for the *Saturday Review,* the *Pall Mall Gazette, Fraser's,* the *Cornhill,* in those years when, as Professor Houghton points out, the most serious readers followed the magazines closely, and the most serious writers were satisfied to write for them. He became well known as an agnostic, a literary critic (most enthusiastic for Dr. Johnson, most scornful of Sterne), an intellectual historian. From that he passed to editing the *Cornhill,* and finally to supervising the *Dictionary of National Biography,* from which he retired as one of the patriarchal figures of British letters of the time.

Here then we have a man who made his acts of allegiance for and against much the same forces in British life as Leavis, and who moved through the same circles of controversy and dispute. What immediately strikes the modern reader of *Some Early Impressions* is its urbanity, its unaggressiveness, its deep acceptance of the institutions and climates in which he lived. This is not a matter of sentimental or whimsical reminiscence; Stephen's was essentially a critical and essentially an honest mind, but the Establishment of his day was not an "Establishment" in our modern sense. He felt unequivocally honored to be taken on the staff of the *Saturday Review;* the Cambridge of Sidgwick, Maitland, and Clerk-Maxwell really sustained and satisfied him. Victorian England offered its Cambridge critic essentially satisfying rewards and conditions; Leavis would not have been a rebel all his life in that society.

I borrow this phrase, "Cambridge critic," from the title of an essay by Q. D. Leavis in *Scrutiny* for March, 1939, provoked by Desmond MacCarthy's Leslie Stephen lecture for 1937. Mrs. Leavis points out Stephen's outspokenness, skepticism, common sense, specificity, his sense of the writer's social position—above all, of course, his moral seriousness—as making him a precursor, indeed the precursor, of her husband and herself. He had been, she says, one of the few people writing after the death of Arnold from whom one could learn something. She and her husband, she claims, have been Cambridge critics in the sense that Stephen had been, in the tradition he had created. MacCarthy, apparently, had apologized for Stephen, as so wrong as a critic though so nice as a man—in his concentration on the intellectual and moral aspects of literature, his ineptness at conveying the emotion the work of art evoked in him, his indifference and insensitiveness to purely aesthetic questions. To all of which, of course, Mrs. Leavis has some very telling answers. And what is most to our purpose, she makes a very convincing case for there being, not two principles, but two modes of English intellectual activity in question here, the Leavises' and MacCarthy's; characterized by the moral sense or the aesthetic sense, the reason or the feelings, adventurous assertion or graceful implication; and she amply demonstrates, by quotation from Stephen, that he too was conscious of the same alternatives (naming themselves to him most clearly as Cambridge and Oxford), and that he most deliberately chose the former. So that if Stephen's is a centrally Victorian mind, it is the Leavises and not the MacCarthys who have represented that tradition today, have recreated it in modern terms.

The Leavises, naturally, are interested in showing that Stephen was like them, their precursor. But from the point of view of this essay it is more important that they are like him, his heirs; the children of his spirit, though not the children of his flesh like Virginia Woolf or Desmond MacCarthy (a personal friend of Stephen's). This is important because as his heirs they are also the heirs of Victorianism, and their rebellion against their contemporaries, and that of Lawrence and Orwell, then takes on a much more than personal or even critical significance, borrows the weight of that complex and stable achievement of intellectual-artistic-social life. It becomes a return to the true spirit of England, a recall of the country to its true identity. They, the oddities, the outcasts, were the true transmitters of tradition.

4. Is There a Present Generation?

The present cultural crisis, then, derives from a quite locatable decision on the part of the last generation to listen not to those among it who carried on the Victorian tradition, but to those who favored a lighter, less personally intense, more elaborate and "traditional" mode. Of course, other factors co-operated, such as the killing or wounding of so many in the war—including wounds as wholly spiritual as E. M. Forster's— and the contrasting survival of every member of Bloomsbury. The more generous and self-offering souls were hurt worse, and Bloomsbury, protected by its skepticism and irony, emerged in 1918 more self-confident and more closely knit than before. These other factors made the decision more wholehearted and widespread, but crucial cases like David Garnett's show that they were not essential. England had already rejected Lawrence and preferred Strachey.

What we are mainly conscious of at the moment is a blank. That ironic and civilized mode of being has exhausted itself. Most of the last generation, Establishment and opposition both, is dead or long silent, and what we read are echoes of them, eccentrics, nonsignificant variants. Even Leavis's work is done, in the sense that, though it still needs spreading in its original form, it needs even more to be reinterpreted and advanced from. Those of us who are about thirty today are in the position of the last generation at that age. We are sure that the last wave has spent its strength, we aren't sure if we are the next wave or just intermediary ripples.

To be a new generation demands a powerful new idea—at least of what was wrong with the past—and more than that. The young writers of the thirties thought that they were a new generation. They had new ideas, wrote new kinds of poems and novels, and were talented enough. But it seems clear now that they were only an interlude, like the writers of the *Yellow Book*. Because their ideas didn't come from deep enough down in them, or answer to anything deep enough in their audience. They played the part of rebels, but within the deeper limits of temperament and sensibility authority had established. The authority remained with the generation of the eighties and nineties, and today the men of the thirties are gone as if they had never been.

Is there then a present generation now? There is, of course, some disturbance, some anger, in the air, and it relies on

Lawrence, Leavis, and Orwell in its attack on the Establishment. So much is hopeful; it indicates both a common and a fruitful tendency. There have been several books recently pointing out Leavis's unique distinction as a British critic of this century. There is *Look Back in Anger,* the most interesting ideas in which come from Orwell and Lawrence. And, much the most important, there is Kingsley Amis, whose work enacts a profound sympathy of temperament with theirs. The central character in his books, when he is talking to himself, in his debates of conscience, and in his comments on modern life, and, to a less extent, in his semi-fantasy adventures, is the same agnostic puritan intellectual as in another century and from another point of view we met in *Some Early Impressions.*

So, if we put all these together, we might hope that a new generation is forming itself, in reaction against the Establishment, and guiding itself by the example of the three great rebels of the last generation. But that would be overinterpretation. Leavis's brilliance as a critic, important though that is, is not the main point about him. Osborne, and most of the Angry Young Men, seem very unsure what they want or are complaining of. Amis is nervous of his own seriousness, and tries to stand for a blunt, blunted manliness, tries to assimilate himself to Fielding. (He does use Fielding as a style for his fantasy life, it's true, but his fantasy is not his best work.) Moreover, he has not yet written a very good novel. But what he has written is the most solid achievement, both aesthetically and ideologically, of this new stirring, this anger.

All one can say is that there is a consciousness of exhaustion and lack which amounts to a positive irritation; and that there are some feeble, ambiguous signs that a new generation is emerging, aware of which are the true and which the false sources of power; and that, by the best reading of those signs, England may be ready to reverse that gesture by which David Garnett turned from D. H. Lawrence to Maynard Keynes on Armistice Day, 1918.

It wasn't until after I had finished this "Background" that I finally traced the intellectual echo that had been baffling me to its source and discovered to whom I was indebted for my image of the essential Englishman. I was rereading Lady Chatterley's Lover after ten years, and I suddenly realized that Oliver Mellors was exactly the man I had described. He had the same unremarkable physical appearance, the same kind of pride and plainness, the same hatred of sentimentality and affectation, the same suspicion of all kinds of polish and gentlemanliness, the same shrewd practicality. He had, of course, been more badly knocked about than most men of this type, and had resented it more; he was "unable to swallow his bile"; but these were merely personal traits. And then I realized that Clifford was a gentleman par excellence, and more than that, a parable of gentlemanliness; with his "conservative anarchism" and his "whispering, murmuring sort of voice, and an ultra-sensitive sort of manner," and his rebellion against his father's love of social forms—a rebellion which issued only in a determined insistence on those forms himself when he inherited; his "wincing sense of the ridiculousness of everything," in nature as well as society, but quite vicious assertion of his de facto rights of possession in property and social position and intellectual ability and everything. Clifford is, quite all-inclusively, the gentlemanly class I have been struggling to define *from the beginning; his paralysis is their paralysis; the blight and withering Connie suffered from him is the blight I tried to analyze in myself; her struggle to be free of him is a parable of mine. But then, of course, I said—the idea developed itself fast—Lady Chatterley's Lover is, most importantly, a book about England. It has always been that aspect of it that has seemed to me the most unambiguously brilliant and moving. The descriptions of Tevershall and Wragby and the flowers in the park capture modern England with an intensity and beauty that nothing else approaches. And the conflict, the alternative posed, either Mellors or Clifford, is of course the essential conflict for Englishmen. There is no other dichotomy in our minds as important as that.*

The battle for the immediate future, in 1930, was already lost, as Lawrence makes plain; the people like Clifford (he belonged to "the young Cambridge group, the group that stood for 'freedom' and flannel trousers, and flannel shirts open at the neck"—in other words, Bloomsbury) were ousting the older generation like Connie's father, the artist, and Clifford's godfather, Squire Winter; and since then they have ensconced themselves in every university chair, every editorial room, every Civil Service post. But thirty years have passed, and they have lost their impetus; their success has made them static. It may be the time for the old irresponsible pendulum motion in human affairs to reassert itself. It may be possible for that to be ridden and diverted into a healthful direction.

At all events, I'm profoundly reassured to find myself coming out by this glorious gateway, to have been under this unidentified direction so long.

The writing of this book has been, as I have said, an exercise in one kind of self-discovery; a process of self-release, a laying of the ghosts that prowled and paralyzed half of my mind so long. So that once finished it might seem that the problem itself

177

is solved, is over and done with; that one could now take one's place in England peacefully, putting one's own interpretation and evaluation on all her phenomena, controlling one's own reactions and responses. But one has to remind oneself that it is not so. The problem was only accidentally personal; essentially it is cultural. However rearranged, relabeled, repriced one's own mind may be, the external world, in which fact and meaning are indissolubly united, remains the same. One is still going to react and respond, however resentfully, under external direction. The college buildings and college legends still offer themselves as a justification of every Cambridge habit; Cambridge history still announces itself a continuity, a tradition, from the thirteenth century down to the present. I know *that in point of fact the English Tripos was instituted after the Great War, by and for the returning Clifford Chatterleys, and that the cultural fact that Cambridge now is can in no sense be traced back any further than the eighties of the last century, when dons were given permission to marry; that anything further back than that is no more relevant to the present climate of education and research there than to the University of North Staffordshire or North Dakota. But if I am standing there, the buildings themselves announce the opposite; they crowd around me, bland and omniscient, like all the ages bearing witness. They don't leave room for any other kind of idea, any other interpretation. Continuity and tradition are lies in England, because they make themselves available to only one group, one sensibility, and that the one turned away from life. One knows, quite clearly and dryly, that they are false, but personal knowledge is ineffective against such multiform social myths. Those lies are reiterated and enacted and celebrated a hundred times a day, by every castle, every guide, every landscape, every cottage, every tea-shoppe, every teacher, every tourist in the country. It's a grim lookout, still.*

178